50 American Pastry Recipes for Home

By: Kelly Johnson

Table of Contents

- Lamingtons
- Anzac Biscuits
- Pavlova
- Meat Pies
- Vanilla Slice (Snot Block)
- Fairy Bread
- Vegemite Scrolls
- Tim Tam Slice
- Vanilla Custard Tarts
- Beef Sausage Rolls
- Passionfruit Sponge Cake
- Chocolate Ripple Cake
- Scones with Jam and Cream
- Lemon Myrtle Cheesecake
- Aussie Damper
- Anzac Slice
- Pumpkin Scones
- Wattleseed Shortbread
- Finger Lime Tart
- Chiko Roll
- Eucalyptus Honey Tart
- Wagon Wheel Slice
- Vanilla Cupcakes with Buttercream Frosting
- Finger Bun
- Bush Bread
- Lemon Meringue Pie
- Lamington Cake
- Vanilla Bean Panna Cotta
- Chocolate Eclairs
- Caramel Slice (Millionaire's Shortbread)
- Apple Crumble Pie
- Wattleseed Brownies
- Lemon Delicious Pudding
- Vanilla Sponge Cake with Passionfruit Icing
- Anzac Cake

- Chocolate Lamingtons
- Date and Walnut Scones
- Caramel Banana Tart
- Apricot Jam Drops
- Lemonade Scones
- Chocolate Custard Tart
- Vanilla Wattleseed Macarons
- Cherry Ripe Slice
- Butterscotch Pudding
- Coffee Scroll
- Coconut Ice
- Custard-filled Profiteroles
- Peanut Butter Chocolate Fudge
- Strawberry and Cream Crepes
- Honey Joys

Lamingtons

Ingredients:

For the sponge cake:

- 1 and 3/4 cups all-purpose flour
- 1 teaspoon baking powder
- 1/4 teaspoon salt
- 1/2 cup unsalted butter, softened
- 3/4 cup granulated sugar
- 2 large eggs
- 1 teaspoon vanilla extract
- 1/2 cup milk

For the chocolate icing:

- 3 and 1/2 cups powdered sugar (icing sugar)
- 1/4 cup unsweetened cocoa powder
- 2 tablespoons unsalted butter, melted
- 1/2 cup milk
- 2 cups desiccated coconut, for coating

Instructions:

1. Prepare the Sponge Cake:
    - Preheat your oven to 350°F (175°C). Grease and flour a 9x13-inch baking pan.
    - In a medium bowl, whisk together the flour, baking powder, and salt. Set aside.
    - In a large mixing bowl, cream together the softened butter and granulated sugar until light and fluffy.
    - Beat in the eggs, one at a time, until well combined. Stir in the vanilla extract.
    - Gradually add the dry ingredients to the wet ingredients, alternating with the milk, mixing until just combined.
    - Pour the batter into the prepared baking pan and spread it out evenly.
    - Bake in the preheated oven for 25-30 minutes, or until a toothpick inserted into the center comes out clean.

- Remove the cake from the oven and let it cool completely in the pan.
2. Cut and Prepare the Cake:
    - Once the cake is completely cooled, turn it out onto a cutting board and cut it into squares, about 2 inches in size.
3. Make the Chocolate Icing:
    - In a large mixing bowl, sift together the powdered sugar and cocoa powder.
    - Add the melted butter and milk to the dry ingredients, whisking until smooth and well combined. If the icing is too thick, you can add a little more milk to reach your desired consistency.
4. Coat the Cake in Chocolate Icing and Coconut:
    - Place the desiccated coconut in a shallow bowl.
    - Using a fork or dipping tool, dip each square of cake into the chocolate icing, coating it completely.
    - Allow any excess icing to drip off, then roll the coated cake square in the desiccated coconut until evenly coated.
    - Place the coated Lamingtons on a wire rack to set.
5. Serve and Enjoy:
    - Once the chocolate icing has set, serve the Lamingtons and enjoy! They can be stored in an airtight container at room temperature for up to 3 days.

These homemade Lamingtons are moist, chocolatey, and delightfully coconut-covered—a true Aussie classic!

Anzac Biscuits

Ingredients:

- 1 cup rolled oats
- 1 cup desiccated coconut
- 1 cup all-purpose flour
- 3/4 cup granulated sugar
- 1/2 cup unsalted butter
- 2 tablespoons golden syrup (or substitute with honey or maple syrup)
- 1 teaspoon baking soda
- 2 tablespoons boiling water

Instructions:

1. Preheat the Oven:
   - Preheat your oven to 350°F (175°C). Line baking sheets with parchment paper or grease them lightly.
2. Mix Dry Ingredients:
   - In a large mixing bowl, combine the rolled oats, desiccated coconut, all-purpose flour, and granulated sugar.
3. Melt Butter and Syrup:
   - In a small saucepan, melt the butter and golden syrup over low heat. Stir until well combined and smooth.
4. Dissolve Baking Soda:
   - In a small bowl, dissolve the baking soda in the boiling water.
5. Combine Wet and Dry Ingredients:
   - Pour the melted butter mixture into the dry ingredients and mix well until everything is thoroughly combined.
6. Add Baking Soda Mixture:
   - Add the dissolved baking soda mixture to the dough and mix until evenly distributed.
7. Shape Dough into Balls:
   - Take tablespoons of the dough and roll them into balls. Place them on the prepared baking sheets, leaving some space between each biscuit as they will spread during baking.
8. Flatten Biscuits:
   - Flatten each ball slightly with the back of a spoon or your fingers. The biscuits should be about 1/2 inch thick.

9. Bake:
    - Bake in the preheated oven for 12-15 minutes, or until the Anzac biscuits are golden brown.
10. Cool:
    - Allow the biscuits to cool on the baking sheets for a few minutes before transferring them to a wire rack to cool completely.
11. Serve:
    - Once cooled, serve and enjoy these delicious Anzac Biscuits with a cup of tea or coffee!

These Anzac Biscuits are crispy on the outside and chewy on the inside, with a delightful combination of oats, coconut, and golden syrup. They're perfect for enjoying as a snack or dessert, and they have a rich history dating back to World War I.

Pavlova

Ingredients:

For the meringue:

- 4 large egg whites, at room temperature
- 1 cup granulated sugar
- 1 teaspoon cornstarch
- 1 teaspoon white vinegar
- 1 teaspoon vanilla extract

For the topping:

- 1 cup heavy cream, cold
- 1 tablespoon granulated sugar
- Fresh fruits (such as strawberries, kiwi, mango, passionfruit, raspberries, or any other fruits of your choice)

Instructions:

1. Preheat the Oven:
    - Preheat your oven to 250°F (120°C). Line a baking sheet with parchment paper.
2. Make the Meringue:
    - In a clean, dry mixing bowl, beat the egg whites on medium speed until soft peaks form.
    - Gradually add the granulated sugar, a spoonful at a time, while continuing to beat the egg whites. Beat until stiff, glossy peaks form.
    - In a small bowl, mix together the cornstarch, white vinegar, and vanilla extract until well combined.
    - Gently fold the cornstarch mixture into the beaten egg whites until evenly incorporated.
3. Shape the Meringue:
    - Spoon the meringue onto the prepared baking sheet and spread it out into a circle, forming a slight indentation in the center to hold the toppings.
4. Bake the Meringue:

- Place the baking sheet in the preheated oven and bake for 1 to 1 1/2 hours, or until the meringue is crisp and dry on the outside. The inside should remain soft and marshmallow-like.
- Turn off the oven and leave the meringue in the oven with the door closed for another hour to cool completely.

5. Prepare the Topping:
    - In a mixing bowl, whip the cold heavy cream and granulated sugar until stiff peaks form.
6. Assemble the Pavlova:
    - Transfer the cooled meringue to a serving platter.
    - Spoon the whipped cream onto the center of the meringue and spread it out evenly.
    - Arrange the fresh fruits on top of the whipped cream.
7. Serve:
    - Slice the pavlova into wedges and serve immediately.

Enjoy the light and airy texture of the pavlova, complemented by the sweetness of the meringue, the creaminess of the whipped cream, and the freshness of the fruits. It's a perfect dessert for any occasion!

Meat Pies

Ingredients:

For the pastry:

- 2 and 1/2 cups all-purpose flour
- 1 teaspoon salt
- 1 cup unsalted butter, chilled and cubed
- 6-8 tablespoons ice water

For the filling:

- 1 tablespoon olive oil
- 1 onion, finely chopped
- 2 cloves garlic, minced
- 1 pound ground beef or lamb
- 2 tablespoons tomato paste
- 1 tablespoon Worcestershire sauce
- 1 teaspoon dried mixed herbs (such as thyme, rosemary, and oregano)
- Salt and pepper, to taste
- 1 cup beef or vegetable broth
- 2 tablespoons all-purpose flour
- 1/2 cup frozen peas (optional)

Instructions:

1. Make the Pastry:
    - In a large mixing bowl, combine the flour and salt. Add the chilled, cubed butter.
    - Use a pastry cutter or your fingertips to rub the butter into the flour until the mixture resembles coarse breadcrumbs.
    - Gradually add the ice water, 1 tablespoon at a time, mixing with a fork until the dough comes together. Be careful not to overwork the dough.
    - Shape the dough into a ball, flatten it into a disk, wrap it in plastic wrap, and refrigerate for at least 30 minutes.
2. Prepare the Filling:

- In a large skillet, heat the olive oil over medium heat. Add the chopped onion and minced garlic, and cook until softened.
- Add the ground beef or lamb to the skillet, breaking it apart with a spoon, and cook until browned.
- Stir in the tomato paste, Worcestershire sauce, dried herbs, salt, and pepper. Cook for another minute.
- Sprinkle the flour over the meat mixture and stir until well combined.
- Gradually pour in the beef or vegetable broth, stirring constantly, until the mixture thickens.
- If using frozen peas, stir them into the filling. Remove the skillet from heat and let the filling cool slightly.

3. Preheat the Oven and Prepare the Pie Crust:
   - Preheat your oven to 400°F (200°C). Grease a 12-cup muffin tin.
   - On a lightly floured surface, roll out the chilled pastry dough to about 1/8-inch thickness. Use a round cutter slightly larger than the muffin tin cups to cut out circles of dough.
4. Assemble the Meat Pies:
   - Place each circle of dough into a muffin tin cup, pressing it gently into the bottom and up the sides.
   - Spoon the meat filling into each pastry-lined cup, filling them almost to the top.
5. Top the Pies:
   - Roll out the remaining pastry dough and cut out smaller circles to use as pie lids. Place a lid on top of each meat-filled cup, pressing the edges to seal.
6. Bake the Pies:
   - Place the muffin tin in the preheated oven and bake for 20-25 minutes, or until the pastry is golden brown and crisp.
7. Cool and Serve:
   - Remove the meat pies from the oven and let them cool in the muffin tin for a few minutes before transferring them to a wire rack to cool completely.
   - Serve the meat pies warm or at room temperature, and enjoy!

These homemade meat pies are flavorful, hearty, and perfect for a satisfying meal or snack. They're a quintessential Aussie comfort food that's sure to be a hit with family and friends!

Vanilla Slice (Snot Block)

Ingredients:

For the pastry:

- 2 sheets of ready-rolled puff pastry
- 1 tablespoon granulated sugar, for sprinkling

For the custard filling:

- 2 cups whole milk
- 1/2 cup granulated sugar
- 1/4 cup cornstarch
- 4 large egg yolks
- 1 teaspoon vanilla extract
- 1 tablespoon unsalted butter

For the icing:

- 1 cup powdered sugar (icing sugar)
- 2 tablespoons hot water
- A few drops of vanilla extract

Instructions:

1. Prepare the Pastry:
    - Preheat your oven to 400°F (200°C). Line a baking sheet with parchment paper.
    - Place one sheet of puff pastry on the prepared baking sheet. Prick the pastry all over with a fork, then sprinkle evenly with 1 tablespoon of granulated sugar. Top with the second sheet of puff pastry.
    - Bake in the preheated oven for 15-20 minutes, or until the pastry is golden brown and puffed up. Remove from the oven and let it cool completely.
2. Make the Custard Filling:
    - In a saucepan, heat the milk over medium heat until it just begins to simmer. Do not let it boil.
    - In a separate mixing bowl, whisk together the granulated sugar, cornstarch, and egg yolks until well combined.

- Slowly pour the hot milk into the egg mixture, whisking constantly to prevent curdling.
- Return the mixture to the saucepan and cook over medium heat, stirring constantly, until thickened.
- Remove the custard from the heat and stir in the vanilla extract and butter until smooth. Let it cool slightly.

3. Assemble the Vanilla Slice:
   - Once the pastry and custard have cooled, carefully cut the pastry sheets in half lengthwise to create four equal-sized rectangles.
   - Place one rectangle of pastry on a serving plate or tray. Spread half of the custard evenly over the pastry. Top with another rectangle of pastry, followed by the remaining custard. Finally, place the last rectangle of pastry on top.
4. Make the Icing:
   - In a small bowl, mix together the powdered sugar, hot water, and vanilla extract until smooth. Adjust the consistency by adding more water if necessary.
5. Ice the Vanilla Slice:
   - Spread the icing evenly over the top layer of pastry.
6. Chill and Serve:
   - Place the vanilla slice in the refrigerator to chill for at least 1 hour, or until the custard has set and the icing has hardened.
   - Once chilled, use a sharp knife to cut the vanilla slice into squares.
   - Serve the vanilla slice cold and enjoy the creamy, vanilla-flavored custard sandwiched between layers of flaky puff pastry!

This Vanilla Slice recipe will give you a taste of this classic Australian dessert, known for its creamy texture and delicious flavor. It's a perfect treat to enjoy with a cup of tea or coffee.

Fairy Bread

Ingredients:

- Sliced white bread
- Unsalted butter, softened
- Rainbow sprinkles or hundreds and thousands (colored sugar sprinkles)

Instructions:

1. Prepare the Bread:
   - Take slices of white bread and trim off the crusts if desired. However, leaving the crusts on is also common and saves waste.
   - Lay the slices of bread out on a clean work surface.
2. Spread Butter:
   - Spread a generous layer of softened unsalted butter over each slice of bread. Ensure that the butter goes all the way to the edges.
3. Add Sprinkles:
   - Sprinkle the rainbow sprinkles or hundreds and thousands generously over the buttered bread slices, ensuring that the sprinkles stick to the butter.
4. Cut and Serve:
   - Once the bread slices are covered in sprinkles, use a sharp knife to cut each slice into triangles, squares, or any shape you prefer.
   - Arrange the Fairy Bread on a serving platter or plate, and it's ready to serve!

Fairy Bread is a fun and colorful treat that's loved by both kids and adults. It's perfect for birthday parties, picnics, or any occasion where you want to add a touch of whimsy to your spread. Enjoy!

Vegemite Scrolls

Ingredients:

- 2 cups self-raising flour
- 1 cup Greek yogurt (or plain yogurt)
- 1/4 cup Vegemite
- 1/2 cup grated cheese (optional)
- 1 tablespoon milk (for brushing)

Instructions:

1. Preheat the Oven:
    - Preheat your oven to 400°F (200°C). Line a baking sheet with parchment paper.
2. Make the Dough:
    - In a large mixing bowl, combine the self-raising flour and Greek yogurt. Mix until a dough forms. If the dough is too sticky, you can add a little extra flour.
3. Roll Out the Dough:
    - Transfer the dough to a lightly floured surface and knead it for a few minutes until smooth.
    - Use a rolling pin to roll out the dough into a rectangle, about 1/4 inch thick.
4. Spread Vegemite:
    - Spread the Vegemite evenly over the surface of the rolled-out dough. Leave a small border around the edges.
5. Add Cheese (Optional):
    - Sprinkle grated cheese evenly over the Vegemite layer, if desired.
6. Roll Up the Dough:
    - Starting from one of the long edges, tightly roll up the dough into a log.
7. Slice the Scrolls:
    - Use a sharp knife to slice the dough log into even-sized scrolls, about 1 inch thick.
8. Arrange on Baking Sheet:
    - Place the scrolls on the prepared baking sheet, leaving a little space between each one.
9. Brush with Milk:

- Brush the tops of the scrolls with a little milk. This will help them brown nicely in the oven.
10. Bake:
    - Bake in the preheated oven for 15-20 minutes, or until the scrolls are golden brown and cooked through.
11. Cool and Serve:
    - Remove the Vegemite Scrolls from the oven and let them cool slightly on the baking sheet before serving.

These Vegemite Scrolls are a delicious and savory snack, perfect for breakfast, brunch, or anytime you're craving a tasty treat. Enjoy them warm or at room temperature!

Tim Tam Slice

Ingredients:

- 200g (7oz) Tim Tam biscuits (any flavor)
- 200g (7oz) dark chocolate, chopped
- 100g (3.5oz) unsalted butter
- 1/4 cup (60ml) condensed milk
- 1 cup (100g) desiccated coconut
- Extra desiccated coconut, for sprinkling (optional)

Instructions:

1. Prepare the Tim Tams:
    - Place the Tim Tam biscuits in a sealable plastic bag. Use a rolling pin to crush the biscuits into small pieces. Set aside.
2. Prepare the Chocolate Mixture:
    - In a heatproof bowl, combine the chopped dark chocolate and unsalted butter. Place the bowl over a saucepan of simmering water (double boiler method) and stir until melted and smooth.
3. Add Condensed Milk:
    - Once the chocolate and butter are melted, remove the bowl from the heat. Stir in the condensed milk until well combined.
4. Combine Ingredients:
    - Add the crushed Tim Tam biscuits and desiccated coconut to the chocolate mixture. Stir until all ingredients are evenly coated.
5. Press into Pan:
    - Line a square baking dish or tray with parchment paper. Transfer the Tim Tam mixture into the lined dish and spread it out evenly, pressing down firmly with the back of a spoon or spatula.
6. Chill:
    - Place the tray in the refrigerator and chill for at least 1 hour, or until set.
7. Slice and Serve:
    - Once the slice is set, remove it from the refrigerator and use a sharp knife to slice it into squares or bars.
    - Optionally, sprinkle extra desiccated coconut over the top before serving.
8. Enjoy:

- Serve the Tim Tam Slice chilled and enjoy the rich chocolatey flavor with the crunchy texture of the Tim Tams!

This Tim Tam Slice recipe is quick and easy to make, and it's a delicious treat for any occasion. Feel free to customize it by using your favorite flavor of Tim Tams or adding extra toppings like chopped nuts or drizzled chocolate.

Vanilla Custard Tarts

Ingredients:

For the pastry:

- 1 1/4 cups all-purpose flour
- 1/4 cup granulated sugar
- 1/2 cup unsalted butter, chilled and cubed
- 1 egg yolk
- 1-2 tablespoons cold water

For the custard filling:

- 2 cups whole milk
- 1/2 cup granulated sugar
- 1/4 cup cornstarch
- 4 large egg yolks
- 1 teaspoon vanilla extract
- Pinch of salt

Instructions:

1. Make the Pastry:
    - In a food processor, combine the flour and sugar. Add the chilled, cubed butter and pulse until the mixture resembles coarse crumbs.
    - Add the egg yolk and 1 tablespoon of cold water. Pulse until the dough comes together, adding more water if needed.
    - Turn the dough out onto a lightly floured surface and knead it briefly until smooth. Wrap in plastic wrap and refrigerate for 30 minutes.
2. Prepare the Custard Filling:
    - In a saucepan, heat the milk over medium heat until it just begins to simmer. Remove from heat.
    - In a mixing bowl, whisk together the granulated sugar, cornstarch, egg yolks, vanilla extract, and a pinch of salt until smooth.
    - Gradually pour the hot milk into the egg mixture, whisking constantly to prevent curdling.

- Return the mixture to the saucepan and cook over medium heat, stirring constantly, until thickened into a custard-like consistency. This should take about 5-7 minutes. Remove from heat and let it cool slightly.
3. Preheat the Oven:
    - Preheat your oven to 375°F (190°C). Grease a 12-cup muffin tin.
4. Roll out the Pastry:
    - On a lightly floured surface, roll out the chilled pastry dough to about 1/8 inch thick. Use a round cutter to cut out circles of dough slightly larger than the muffin tin cups.
5. Line the Muffin Tin:
    - Press the pastry circles into the muffin tin cups, pressing them gently against the bottom and sides.
6. Fill with Custard:
    - Spoon the slightly cooled custard filling into each pastry-lined cup, filling them almost to the top.
7. Bake the Tarts:
    - Place the muffin tin in the preheated oven and bake for 20-25 minutes, or until the pastry is golden brown and the custard is set.
8. Cool and Serve:
    - Remove the custard tarts from the oven and let them cool in the muffin tin for a few minutes before transferring them to a wire rack to cool completely.
    - Serve the vanilla custard tarts at room temperature, and enjoy their creamy, indulgent flavor!

These Vanilla Custard Tarts are a delightful dessert that's sure to impress your family and friends. They're perfect for any occasion, from afternoon tea to special celebrations.

Beef Sausage Rolls

Ingredients:

For the filling:

- 1 pound (450g) ground beef
- 1 small onion, finely chopped
- 2 cloves garlic, minced
- 1/2 cup breadcrumbs
- 1 egg
- 2 tablespoons tomato sauce (ketchup)
- 1 tablespoon Worcestershire sauce
- 1 teaspoon dried mixed herbs (such as thyme, rosemary, and oregano)
- Salt and pepper to taste

For the pastry:

- 1 package of puff pastry (about 17.3 ounces or 490g), thawed if frozen
- 1 egg, beaten (for egg wash)

Instructions:

1. Preheat the Oven:
    - Preheat your oven to 400°F (200°C). Line a baking sheet with parchment paper.
2. Make the Filling:
    - In a large mixing bowl, combine the ground beef, finely chopped onion, minced garlic, breadcrumbs, egg, tomato sauce, Worcestershire sauce, dried herbs, salt, and pepper. Mix until well combined.
3. Prepare the Pastry:
    - Roll out the puff pastry on a lightly floured surface into a large rectangle, about 1/4 inch thick.
4. Shape the Sausage Rolls:
    - Spoon the beef mixture along one edge of the pastry, forming a long sausage shape. Leave a border of pastry along the edge.
    - Roll up the pastry tightly over the filling, sealing the edge by pressing lightly.
5. Cut and Seal the Rolls:

- Use a sharp knife to cut the long roll into smaller pieces, each about 2-3 inches long.
- Place the rolls seam side down on the prepared baking sheet. Press the edges lightly to seal.

6. Brush with Egg Wash:
   - Brush the tops of the sausage rolls with beaten egg. This will give them a golden brown color when baked.
7. Bake the Sausage Rolls:
   - Place the baking sheet in the preheated oven and bake for 20-25 minutes, or until the pastry is golden brown and cooked through, and the beef filling is cooked.
8. Cool and Serve:
   - Remove the beef sausage rolls from the oven and let them cool slightly on the baking sheet before serving.
   - Serve the sausage rolls warm, with tomato sauce or your favorite dipping sauce on the side.

These beef sausage rolls are perfect for parties, picnics, or as a delicious snack or appetizer any time of the day. They're flavorful, comforting, and sure to be a hit with everyone!

Passionfruit Sponge Cake

Ingredients:

For the sponge cake:

- 4 large eggs, at room temperature
- 1 cup granulated sugar
- 1 teaspoon vanilla extract
- 1/2 cup milk
- 1 cup all-purpose flour
- 1 teaspoon baking powder
- Pinch of salt

For the passionfruit filling:

- 1/2 cup passionfruit pulp (fresh or canned)
- 1/4 cup granulated sugar
- 1 tablespoon cornstarch
- 1/4 cup water

For the whipped cream:

- 1 cup heavy cream, chilled
- 2 tablespoons powdered sugar
- 1 teaspoon vanilla extract

Instructions:

1. Preheat the Oven:
    - Preheat your oven to 350°F (175°C). Grease and flour two 9-inch round cake pans.
2. Make the Sponge Cake:
    - In a large mixing bowl, beat the eggs and granulated sugar together with an electric mixer until pale and fluffy.
    - Mix in the vanilla extract.
    - In a separate bowl, sift together the flour, baking powder, and salt.
    - Gradually add the dry ingredients to the egg mixture, alternating with the milk, and mixing until just combined.

- Divide the batter evenly between the prepared cake pans and smooth the tops with a spatula.
- Bake in the preheated oven for 20-25 minutes, or until the cakes are lightly golden and a toothpick inserted into the center comes out clean.
- Remove the cakes from the oven and let them cool in the pans for 10 minutes before transferring them to a wire rack to cool completely.

3. Make the Passionfruit Filling:
   - In a small saucepan, combine the passionfruit pulp, granulated sugar, cornstarch, and water.
   - Cook over medium heat, stirring constantly, until the mixture thickens into a sauce. Remove from heat and let it cool completely.

4. Make the Whipped Cream:
   - In a chilled mixing bowl, beat the heavy cream, powdered sugar, and vanilla extract together until stiff peaks form.

5. Assemble the Cake:
   - Place one of the cooled sponge cakes on a serving plate.
   - Spread the passionfruit filling evenly over the top of the cake.
   - Spread a layer of whipped cream over the passionfruit filling.
   - Place the second sponge cake on top and press down gently.
   - Frost the top of the cake with the remaining whipped cream.

6. Serve and Enjoy:
   - Chill the cake in the refrigerator for at least 1 hour before serving to allow the flavors to meld.
   - Slice and serve the passionfruit sponge cake, and enjoy its light and fluffy texture with the tangy sweetness of the passionfruit filling!

This passionfruit sponge cake is a delightful dessert that's perfect for any occasion, from afternoon tea to special celebrations. Enjoy its tropical flavor and airy texture with friends and family!

Chocolate Ripple Cake

Ingredients:

- 1 package (200g) of Chocolate Ripple biscuits (or any chocolate wafer cookies)
- 1 1/2 cups (375ml) of heavy whipping cream
- 1 tablespoon of cocoa powder (optional)
- 1 tablespoon of powdered sugar (optional)
- 1 teaspoon of vanilla extract (optional)
- Chocolate shavings, cocoa powder, or crushed biscuits for garnish (optional)

Instructions:

1. Prepare the Cream:
    - In a large mixing bowl, pour in the heavy whipping cream. Add cocoa powder, powdered sugar, and vanilla extract if desired for extra flavor. These ingredients are optional but can enhance the taste of the whipped cream.
2. Whip the Cream:
    - Using a hand mixer or a stand mixer fitted with the whisk attachment, whip the cream until stiff peaks form. Be careful not to overwhip the cream.
3. Assemble the Cake:
    - Take a serving plate or a cake stand where you'll assemble the cake.
    - Spread a small amount of whipped cream on the plate to act as a base for the cake. This will help the biscuits stick to the plate.
    - Take one Chocolate Ripple biscuit and spread a thin layer of whipped cream on one side.
    - Place the biscuit vertically on the plate, cream side down. The whipped cream helps the biscuits stick together.
    - Repeat this process, spreading whipped cream on each biscuit and stacking them vertically to form a log or roll shape. Continue until you've used all the biscuits or reached your desired size for the cake.
4. Cover with Whipped Cream:
    - Once you've assembled the cake, cover the entire log with the remaining whipped cream. Use a spatula to spread the cream evenly over the surface and sides of the cake.
5. Decorate:
    - Garnish the cake with chocolate shavings, cocoa powder, or crushed biscuits for added texture and presentation.

6. Chill:
    - Place the Chocolate Ripple Cake in the refrigerator to chill for at least 4 hours or overnight. Chilling allows the biscuits to soften and absorb the cream, resulting in a deliciously moist and creamy cake.
7. Serve:
    - Once chilled, slice the cake using a sharp knife and serve. Enjoy the creamy, chocolatey goodness of this simple yet delicious dessert!

Chocolate Ripple Cake is perfect for any occasion, from casual gatherings to special celebrations. It's easy to make and always a crowd-pleaser!

Scones with Jam and Cream

Ingredients:

- 2 cups (250g) all-purpose flour, plus extra for dusting
- 1/4 cup (50g) granulated sugar
- 1 tablespoon baking powder
- 1/2 teaspoon salt
- 1/3 cup (75g) unsalted butter, cold and cubed
- 1/2 cup (120ml) milk
- 1 large egg
- Jam (such as strawberry, raspberry, or apricot) for serving
- Clotted cream or whipped cream for serving

Instructions:

1. Preheat the Oven:
    - Preheat your oven to 400°F (200°C). Line a baking sheet with parchment paper.
2. Prepare the Scone Dough:
    - In a large mixing bowl, whisk together the flour, sugar, baking powder, and salt.
    - Add the cold cubed butter to the flour mixture. Using your fingertips or a pastry cutter, rub the butter into the flour until the mixture resembles coarse breadcrumbs.
3. Add Liquid Ingredients:
    - In a separate bowl, whisk together the milk and egg until well combined.
    - Make a well in the center of the dry ingredients and pour in the milk mixture.
    - Using a fork or a wooden spoon, gently mix until the dough comes together. Be careful not to overmix.
4. Shape the Scones:
    - Transfer the dough onto a lightly floured surface. Gently pat the dough into a circle about 1 inch (2.5cm) thick.
    - Use a floured round cutter (about 2.5 inches or 6cm in diameter) to cut out scones from the dough. Press straight down without twisting the cutter to ensure the scones rise evenly.
    - Place the scones on the prepared baking sheet, leaving a little space between each one.

5. Bake the Scones:
    - Brush the tops of the scones with a little milk or beaten egg for a golden finish (optional).
    - Bake in the preheated oven for 12-15 minutes, or until the scones are golden brown and cooked through. They should sound hollow when tapped on the bottom.
6. Serve:
    - Once baked, transfer the scones to a wire rack to cool slightly.
    - To serve, split the scones in half and spread with jam and clotted cream or whipped cream. Traditionally, the jam is spread first, followed by a dollop of cream on top.
7. Enjoy:
    - Serve the scones warm or at room temperature, and enjoy them with a cup of tea or coffee for a delightful treat!

These homemade scones with jam and cream are best enjoyed fresh on the day they're made, but you can also store any leftovers in an airtight container for a day or two.

Lemon Myrtle Cheesecake

Ingredients:

For the crust:

- 1 1/2 cups graham cracker crumbs
- 1/4 cup granulated sugar
- 6 tablespoons unsalted butter, melted

For the filling:

- 24 oz (680g) cream cheese, softened
- 1 cup granulated sugar
- 3 large eggs
- 1/4 cup sour cream
- 1/4 cup heavy cream
- 2 tablespoons all-purpose flour
- 1 tablespoon lemon myrtle powder
- Zest of 1 lemon
- 1 teaspoon vanilla extract

For the topping:

- 1 cup sour cream
- 2 tablespoons granulated sugar
- Zest of 1 lemon

Instructions:

1. Preheat the Oven:
    - Preheat your oven to 325°F (160°C). Grease a 9-inch springform pan and line the bottom with parchment paper.
2. Make the Crust:
    - In a mixing bowl, combine the graham cracker crumbs, sugar, and melted butter. Press the mixture firmly into the bottom of the prepared pan. Use

the bottom of a glass or measuring cup to ensure a compact and even layer.
3. Prepare the Filling:
    - In a large mixing bowl, beat the cream cheese and sugar together until smooth and creamy.
    - Add the eggs one at a time, beating well after each addition.
    - Mix in the sour cream, heavy cream, flour, lemon myrtle powder, lemon zest, and vanilla extract until fully incorporated and smooth. Be careful not to overmix.
4. Bake the Cheesecake:
    - Pour the filling over the prepared crust in the springform pan. Smooth the top with a spatula.
    - Place the cheesecake in the preheated oven and bake for 45-50 minutes, or until the edges are set and the center is slightly jiggly.
    - Remove the cheesecake from the oven and let it cool in the pan on a wire rack for 10 minutes.
5. Prepare the Topping:
    - In a small bowl, mix together the sour cream, sugar, and lemon zest until smooth.
    - Carefully spread the sour cream topping over the slightly cooled cheesecake.
6. Chill the Cheesecake:
    - Once topped, return the cheesecake to the oven and bake for an additional 5 minutes.
    - Remove the cheesecake from the oven and let it cool completely in the pan on a wire rack.
    - Once cooled to room temperature, refrigerate the cheesecake for at least 4 hours or overnight to set.
7. Serve:
    - Before serving, carefully remove the sides of the springform pan.
    - Slice the cheesecake and serve chilled. Optionally, garnish with fresh lemon slices or additional lemon zest.

Enjoy the refreshing and aromatic flavor of this lemon myrtle cheesecake as a delightful dessert for any occasion!

Aussie Damper

Ingredients:

- 3 cups self-rising flour
- 1 teaspoon salt
- 1 cup milk (you can also use water or beer for a different flavor)
- 2 tablespoons butter or vegetable oil

Optional Additions:

- 2 tablespoons sugar (for a sweeter damper)
- 1/2 cup grated cheese
- 2 tablespoons dried herbs (such as rosemary, thyme, or oregano)
- 1/4 cup chopped cooked bacon or ham

Instructions:

1. Preheat the Oven:
    - Preheat your oven to 400°F (200°C). Lightly grease a baking tray or line it with parchment paper.
2. Prepare the Dough:
    - In a large mixing bowl, sift the self-rising flour and salt together. If you're adding sugar, cheese, herbs, or other optional ingredients, mix them in at this stage.
    - Make a well in the center of the flour mixture and pour in the milk. Use a wooden spoon or your hands to mix until a dough forms. Be careful not to overwork the dough.
3. Shape the Damper:
    - Turn the dough out onto a lightly floured surface. Shape it into a round loaf, about 1 inch (2.5cm) thick. You can also shape it into smaller individual damper rounds if you prefer.
4. Bake the Damper:
    - Place the shaped damper on the prepared baking tray. Use a sharp knife to score a cross into the top of the damper, about halfway through the dough.
    - Brush the top of the damper with melted butter or vegetable oil.
    - Bake in the preheated oven for 30-40 minutes, or until the damper is golden brown and sounds hollow when tapped on the bottom.

5. Serve:
    - Once baked, transfer the damper to a wire rack to cool slightly.
    - Serve the Aussie damper warm or at room temperature, sliced and spread with butter or your favorite toppings such as jam, honey, or Vegemite.

Aussie damper is best enjoyed fresh on the day it's made, but you can also wrap any leftovers in foil and reheat them in the oven or over a campfire the next day. Enjoy this rustic Australian bread as a delicious and versatile treat!

Anzac Slice

Ingredients:

- 1 cup rolled oats
- 1 cup desiccated coconut
- 1 cup all-purpose flour
- 1/2 cup brown sugar
- 1/2 cup unsalted butter, melted
- 2 tablespoons golden syrup or honey
- 1 teaspoon baking soda
- 2 tablespoons boiling water

Instructions:

1. Preheat the Oven:
    - Preheat your oven to 350°F (175°C). Grease and line a 9x9 inch baking pan with parchment paper, leaving some overhang on the sides for easy removal.
2. Prepare the Dry Ingredients:
    - In a large mixing bowl, combine the rolled oats, desiccated coconut, all-purpose flour, and brown sugar. Mix well to combine.
3. Prepare the Wet Ingredients:
    - In a small saucepan, melt the unsalted butter over low heat. Once melted, add the golden syrup or honey and stir until combined.
4. Combine the Ingredients:
    - In a small bowl, dissolve the baking soda in the boiling water. Add this mixture to the melted butter and golden syrup. Stir well.
5. Mix the Batter:
    - Pour the wet ingredients into the bowl of dry ingredients. Stir until everything is well combined and forms a sticky dough.
6. Press into Pan:
    - Transfer the dough into the prepared baking pan. Use a spatula or your hands to press the dough evenly into the pan, smoothing the surface.
7. Bake:
    - Place the pan in the preheated oven and bake for 20-25 minutes, or until the slice is golden brown on top and firm to the touch.
8. Cool and Slice:

- Remove the pan from the oven and allow the Anzac slice to cool in the pan for about 10 minutes. Then, transfer it to a wire rack to cool completely.

9. Serve:
    - Once cooled, use a sharp knife to slice the Anzac slice into squares or bars. Serve and enjoy!

This Anzac slice is perfect for morning or afternoon tea, picnics, or as a tasty treat any time of the day. It's a delicious twist on a classic Australian favorite!

Pumpkin Scones

Ingredients:

- 2 cups all-purpose flour
- 1/4 cup granulated sugar
- 1 tablespoon baking powder
- 1/2 teaspoon salt
- 1 teaspoon ground cinnamon
- 1/2 teaspoon ground nutmeg
- 1/4 teaspoon ground ginger
- 1/4 teaspoon ground cloves
- 1/2 cup cold unsalted butter, cut into small pieces
- 1/2 cup pumpkin puree (canned or homemade)
- 1/4 cup milk
- 1 large egg
- 1 teaspoon vanilla extract

For brushing:

- 1 tablespoon milk
- 1 tablespoon granulated sugar

Instructions:

1. Preheat the Oven:
    - Preheat your oven to 400°F (200°C). Line a baking sheet with parchment paper.
2. Prepare the Dry Ingredients:
    - In a large mixing bowl, whisk together the flour, sugar, baking powder, salt, cinnamon, nutmeg, ginger, and cloves until well combined.
3. Cut in the Butter:
    - Add the cold butter pieces to the dry ingredients. Use a pastry cutter or two knives to cut the butter into the flour mixture until it resembles coarse crumbs.
4. Mix Wet Ingredients:
    - In a separate bowl, whisk together the pumpkin puree, milk, egg, and vanilla extract until smooth.
5. Combine Wet and Dry Ingredients:

- Pour the wet ingredients into the dry ingredients. Use a wooden spoon or spatula to gently mix until a dough forms. Be careful not to overmix.

6. Shape the Scones:
    - Turn the dough out onto a lightly floured surface. Gently pat the dough into a circle about 1 inch (2.5 cm) thick.
    - Use a floured round cutter (about 2-3 inches or 5-7.5 cm in diameter) to cut out scones from the dough. Press straight down without twisting the cutter to ensure the scones rise evenly.
7. Bake the Scones:
    - Place the scones on the prepared baking sheet. Brush the tops of the scones with milk and sprinkle with sugar.
    - Bake in the preheated oven for 12-15 minutes, or until the scones are golden brown and cooked through.
8. Serve:
    - Once baked, transfer the scones to a wire rack to cool slightly.
    - Serve warm with butter, jam, or whipped cream, and enjoy!

These pumpkin scones are perfect for breakfast, brunch, or a cozy afternoon tea. They're moist, tender, and full of warm, autumnal flavors. Enjoy!

Wattleseed Shortbread

Ingredients:

- 1 cup (225g) unsalted butter, softened
- 1/2 cup (100g) granulated sugar
- 2 cups (250g) all-purpose flour
- 1/4 cup (30g) cornstarch
- 2 tablespoons wattleseed powder
- Pinch of salt

Instructions:

1. Preheat the Oven:
    - Preheat your oven to 325°F (160°C). Line a baking sheet with parchment paper.
2. Prepare the Wattleseed:
    - If using whole wattleseed, grind it to a fine powder using a spice grinder or mortar and pestle. Alternatively, you can purchase wattleseed powder from specialty stores.
3. Cream the Butter and Sugar:
    - In a large mixing bowl, cream together the softened butter and granulated sugar until light and fluffy.
4. Add Dry Ingredients:
    - Sift the all-purpose flour, cornstarch, wattleseed powder, and a pinch of salt into the bowl with the creamed butter and sugar.
5. Mix to Form Dough:
    - Use a spatula or your hands to mix the dry ingredients into the butter and sugar until a dough forms. Be careful not to overmix.
6. Shape the Dough:
    - Transfer the dough onto a lightly floured surface. Gently knead the dough until smooth.
7. Roll Out and Cut the Dough:
    - Roll out the dough to about 1/4 inch (6mm) thickness. Use cookie cutters to cut out shapes, or simply slice the dough into squares or rectangles.
8. Bake the Shortbread:
    - Place the shortbread shapes on the prepared baking sheet, leaving a little space between each one.
    - Prick the tops of the shortbread with a fork to create a decorative pattern.

- Bake in the preheated oven for 12-15 minutes, or until the edges are lightly golden.
9. Cool and Serve:
    - Remove the shortbread from the oven and let them cool on the baking sheet for a few minutes before transferring them to a wire rack to cool completely.
10. Store:
    - Once cooled, store the wattleseed shortbread in an airtight container at room temperature for up to a week.

Enjoy these wattleseed shortbread cookies with a cup of tea or coffee for a delicious treat with a distinctive Australian flavor!

Finger Lime Tart

Ingredients:

For the crust:

- 1 1/2 cups graham cracker crumbs (about 10-12 whole graham crackers)
- 6 tablespoons unsalted butter, melted
- 1/4 cup granulated sugar

For the filling:

- 1 cup finger lime pearls (removed from the fruit)
- 1/2 cup granulated sugar
- 1/4 cup fresh lime juice
- Zest of 1 lime
- 4 large eggs
- 1/2 cup heavy cream

For garnish (optional):

- Whipped cream
- Additional finger lime pearls
- Lime zest

Instructions:

1. Preheat the Oven:
    - Preheat your oven to 350°F (175°C).
2. Prepare the Crust:
    - In a mixing bowl, combine the graham cracker crumbs, melted butter, and granulated sugar until evenly moistened.
    - Press the mixture into the bottom and up the sides of a 9-inch tart pan with a removable bottom.
    - Bake the crust in the preheated oven for 10-12 minutes, or until lightly golden brown. Remove from the oven and let it cool while you prepare the filling.
3. Prepare the Filling:
    - In a blender or food processor, combine the finger lime pearls, granulated sugar, lime juice, and lime zest. Blend until smooth.

- Add the eggs and heavy cream to the blender and blend again until well combined and smooth.
4. Bake the Tart:
    - Pour the filling into the pre-baked crust.
    - Place the tart pan on a baking sheet and transfer it to the oven.
    - Bake for 25-30 minutes, or until the filling is set but still slightly jiggly in the center.
    - Remove the tart from the oven and let it cool to room temperature. Then, refrigerate it for at least 2 hours, or until chilled and set.
5. Serve:
    - Once chilled, carefully remove the tart from the pan and place it on a serving plate.
    - Garnish with whipped cream, additional finger lime pearls, and lime zest, if desired.
    - Slice and serve the finger lime tart, and enjoy the burst of citrus flavor!

This finger lime tart is a refreshing and visually stunning dessert that's sure to impress your guests. It's perfect for special occasions or whenever you want to showcase the unique flavors of finger limes.

Chiko Roll

Ingredients:

For the filling:

- 1 tablespoon vegetable oil
- 1 onion, finely chopped
- 2 cloves garlic, minced
- 1 carrot, grated
- 1 celery stalk, finely chopped
- 1/2 pound (225g) ground beef or pork
- 1 tablespoon Worcestershire sauce
- 1 tablespoon tomato sauce (ketchup)
- 1 tablespoon soy sauce
- Salt and pepper to taste
- 1 cup shredded cabbage

For the pastry:

- 6 sheets of spring roll wrappers (about 8x8 inches or 20x20cm each)
- 1 egg, beaten (for sealing the rolls)
- Vegetable oil, for deep frying

Instructions:

1. Prepare the Filling:
    - Heat vegetable oil in a large skillet over medium heat. Add the chopped onion and garlic, and sauté until softened.
    - Add the grated carrot and chopped celery, and cook for a few minutes until they begin to soften.
    - Add the ground meat to the skillet and cook until browned, breaking it up with a spoon as it cooks.
    - Stir in the Worcestershire sauce, tomato sauce, soy sauce, salt, and pepper. Cook for another minute or two.
    - Add the shredded cabbage to the skillet and cook until wilted. Remove from heat and let the filling cool slightly.

2. Assemble the Chiko Rolls:
   - Lay a spring roll wrapper on a clean work surface with one corner pointing towards you.
   - Place a spoonful of the filling along the bottom edge of the wrapper, leaving some space at the sides.
   - Fold the bottom corner of the wrapper over the filling, then fold the sides in towards the center, and roll tightly to enclose the filling. Brush the top corner with beaten egg to seal the roll.
   - Repeat with the remaining wrappers and filling until all the rolls are assembled.
3. Deep Fry the Chiko Rolls:
   - Heat vegetable oil in a deep fryer or large pot to 350°F (180°C).
   - Carefully add the Chiko Rolls to the hot oil in batches, making sure not to overcrowd the fryer.
   - Fry the rolls for 5-7 minutes, or until they are golden brown and crispy.
   - Use a slotted spoon to transfer the fried rolls to a plate lined with paper towels to drain excess oil.
4. Serve:
   - Serve the Chiko Rolls hot with your favorite dipping sauce, such as sweet chili sauce or tomato sauce (ketchup).
   - Enjoy the crispy and savory goodness of homemade Chiko Rolls as a delicious snack or meal!

Note: The filling ingredients can be adjusted to suit your taste preferences. You can also add additional vegetables or seasonings as desired.

Eucalyptus Honey Tart

Ingredients:

For the crust:

- 1 1/2 cups all-purpose flour
- 1/4 cup granulated sugar
- 1/2 cup unsalted butter, cold and cubed
- 1 egg yolk
- 2-3 tablespoons cold water

For the filling:

- 1 cup eucalyptus honey
- 1/2 cup heavy cream
- 2 large eggs
- 1 teaspoon vanilla extract
- Pinch of salt

Instructions:

1. Prepare the Crust:
    - In a food processor, combine the flour and granulated sugar. Add the cold, cubed butter and pulse until the mixture resembles coarse crumbs.
    - Add the egg yolk and cold water, one tablespoon at a time, and pulse until the dough comes together.
    - Turn the dough out onto a lightly floured surface and knead briefly until smooth. Shape it into a disk, wrap in plastic wrap, and refrigerate for at least 30 minutes.
2. Roll Out the Crust:
    - Preheat your oven to 375°F (190°C). On a lightly floured surface, roll out the chilled dough into a circle large enough to line a 9-inch tart pan. Press the dough into the bottom and up the sides of the pan. Trim any excess dough.
3. Pre-bake the Crust:
    - Line the tart shell with parchment paper and fill it with pie weights or dried beans. Bake in the preheated oven for 15 minutes.

- Remove the parchment paper and weights, and bake for an additional 5 minutes, or until the crust is lightly golden. Remove from the oven and let cool slightly.
4. Prepare the Filling:
   - In a saucepan, warm the eucalyptus honey over low heat until it becomes more liquid and easier to work with. Be careful not to boil it.
   - In a mixing bowl, whisk together the warm honey, heavy cream, eggs, vanilla extract, and a pinch of salt until well combined.
5. Assemble and Bake the Tart:
   - Pour the honey filling into the pre-baked tart shell. Place the tart pan on a baking sheet to catch any drips.
   - Bake in the preheated oven for 25-30 minutes, or until the filling is set and slightly puffed.
   - Remove from the oven and let the tart cool completely before serving.
6. Serve:
   - Once cooled, slice and serve the eucalyptus honey tart at room temperature. Optionally, garnish with a drizzle of warmed eucalyptus honey or a dollop of whipped cream.

Enjoy the unique and aromatic flavor of this eucalyptus honey tart as a delightful dessert or treat!

Wagon Wheel Slice

Ingredients:

For the base:

- 200g (about 7 oz) plain sweet biscuits (like digestive biscuits or graham crackers)
- 100g (about 3.5 oz) unsalted butter, melted

For the marshmallow layer:

- 200g (about 7 oz) pink and white marshmallows
- 2 tablespoons water

For the chocolate coating:

- 200g (about 7 oz) milk chocolate, chopped
- 1 tablespoon vegetable oil

For the filling:

- 150g (about 5 oz) raspberry jam

Instructions:

1. Prepare the Base:
    - Line a 20cm x 20cm (8-inch x 8-inch) square baking dish with parchment paper, leaving some overhang on the sides for easy removal later.
    - Crush the biscuits into fine crumbs. You can do this by placing them in a resealable plastic bag and crushing them with a rolling pin or by using a food processor.
    - Mix the melted butter with the biscuit crumbs until well combined.
    - Press the mixture evenly into the bottom of the prepared baking dish. Use the back of a spoon or your fingers to press it down firmly. Place the dish in the refrigerator to set while you prepare the marshmallow layer.
2. Prepare the Marshmallow Layer:

- In a heatproof bowl set over a pot of simmering water (or using a double boiler), combine the marshmallows and water. Stir until the marshmallows are completely melted and smooth.
- Pour the melted marshmallow mixture over the biscuit base and spread it out evenly using a spatula. Return the dish to the refrigerator to chill while you prepare the chocolate coating.

3. Prepare the Chocolate Coating:
   - In a microwave-safe bowl or using a double boiler, melt the milk chocolate and vegetable oil together until smooth, stirring occasionally.
   - Remove the baking dish from the refrigerator and pour the melted chocolate over the marshmallow layer, spreading it out evenly to cover the surface.
4. Add the Filling:
   - Warm the raspberry jam slightly in the microwave or on the stovetop until it becomes more spreadable.
   - Carefully spread the raspberry jam over the melted chocolate layer.
5. Chill and Set:
   - Place the baking dish back in the refrigerator and chill the slice for at least 2 hours, or until the chocolate is set.
6. Slice and Serve:
   - Once set, use the parchment paper overhang to lift the Wagon Wheel Slice out of the baking dish.
   - Use a sharp knife to slice the slice into squares or bars.
   - Serve and enjoy!

This Wagon Wheel Slice is a delightful treat that combines the flavors of biscuits, marshmallows, raspberry jam, and chocolate into one irresistible dessert.

Vanilla Cupcakes with Buttercream Frosting

Ingredients:

For the vanilla cupcakes:

- 1 1/2 cups all-purpose flour
- 1 1/2 teaspoons baking powder
- 1/4 teaspoon salt
- 1/2 cup unsalted butter, softened
- 1 cup granulated sugar
- 2 large eggs, room temperature
- 2 teaspoons vanilla extract
- 1/2 cup whole milk, room temperature

For the buttercream frosting:

- 1 cup unsalted butter, softened
- 3-4 cups powdered sugar
- 2-3 tablespoons heavy cream or milk
- 1 teaspoon vanilla extract
- Pinch of salt

Instructions:

1. Preheat the oven: Preheat your oven to 350°F (175°C). Line a muffin tin with cupcake liners.
2. Make the cupcakes:
    - In a medium bowl, whisk together the flour, baking powder, and salt. Set aside.
    - In a large mixing bowl, cream together the softened butter and granulated sugar until light and fluffy.
    - Add the eggs, one at a time, beating well after each addition. Stir in the vanilla extract.
    - Gradually add the dry ingredients to the wet ingredients, alternating with the milk, beginning and ending with the dry ingredients. Mix until just combined.
    - Fill each cupcake liner about two-thirds full with the batter.

- Bake for 18-20 minutes, or until a toothpick inserted into the center of a cupcake comes out clean.
- Remove from the oven and transfer the cupcakes to a wire rack to cool completely before frosting.
3. Make the buttercream frosting:
    - In a large mixing bowl, beat the softened butter on medium speed until creamy and smooth.
    - Gradually add the powdered sugar, one cup at a time, beating well after each addition.
    - Add the vanilla extract, salt, and heavy cream or milk. Beat on medium-high speed for 3-5 minutes, or until the frosting is light and fluffy. If the frosting is too thick, add more cream or milk, 1 tablespoon at a time, until desired consistency is reached.
4. Frost the cupcakes:
    - Once the cupcakes are completely cooled, use a piping bag fitted with your desired tip to frost the cupcakes with the buttercream frosting.
    - Decorate the frosted cupcakes with sprinkles, if desired.
5. Serve and enjoy!

These vanilla cupcakes with buttercream frosting are perfect for birthdays, parties, or any special occasion. They're simple to make and always a crowd-pleaser!

Finger Bun

Ingredients:

For the dough:

- 4 cups all-purpose flour
- 1/4 cup granulated sugar
- 1 teaspoon salt
- 2 1/4 teaspoons active dry yeast (1 packet)
- 1 cup warm milk (about 110°F or 45°C)
- 1/4 cup unsalted butter, melted
- 1 large egg

For the filling:

- 1/2 cup raisins or sultanas
- 1/4 cup unsalted butter, softened
- 1/4 cup granulated sugar
- 2 teaspoons ground cinnamon

For the icing:

- 1 cup powdered sugar (icing sugar)
- 1-2 tablespoons milk
- 1/2 teaspoon vanilla extract
- Desiccated coconut, for sprinkling (optional)

Instructions:

1. Prepare the Dough:
    - In a large mixing bowl, combine the warm milk and granulated sugar. Sprinkle the yeast over the mixture and let it sit for about 5-10 minutes, until foamy.
    - Add the melted butter and egg to the yeast mixture and whisk until well combined.

- Gradually add the flour and salt to the wet ingredients, stirring until a soft dough forms.
- Turn the dough out onto a lightly floured surface and knead for about 5-7 minutes, until smooth and elastic. Place the dough in a greased bowl, cover with a clean towel or plastic wrap, and let it rise in a warm place for about 1 hour, or until doubled in size.

2. Prepare the Filling:
   - In a small bowl, combine the softened butter, granulated sugar, and ground cinnamon to make the filling. Set aside.
   - If using raisins or sultanas, you can either mix them into the filling or sprinkle them over the dough before rolling.

3. Assemble the Finger Buns:
   - Punch down the risen dough and turn it out onto a lightly floured surface. Roll it out into a rectangle, about 12x18 inches.
   - Spread the filling evenly over the dough, leaving a small border around the edges.
   - Starting from one long edge, roll the dough tightly into a log. Pinch the seam to seal.
   - Use a sharp knife to cut the log into 12 equal pieces. Place the pieces cut-side up in a greased baking dish, leaving a little space between each bun.
   - Cover the buns loosely with plastic wrap and let them rise for another 30-45 minutes, until puffed up.

4. Bake the Finger Buns:
   - Preheat your oven to 350°F (175°C). Once the buns have risen, remove the plastic wrap and bake them in the preheated oven for 20-25 minutes, until golden brown and cooked through.
   - Remove the buns from the oven and let them cool slightly in the baking dish.

5. Prepare the Icing:
   - In a small bowl, whisk together the powdered sugar, milk, and vanilla extract to make the icing. Adjust the consistency by adding more milk if too thick or more powdered sugar if too thin.
   - Drizzle the icing over the warm finger buns and sprinkle with desiccated coconut, if desired.

6. Serve and Enjoy:
   - Let the finger buns cool completely in the baking dish before serving. Enjoy these delicious homemade treats with a cup of tea or coffee!

These homemade finger buns are soft, fluffy, and filled with sweet cinnamon goodness—a perfect treat for any time of day!

Bush Bread

Ingredients:

- 2 cups whole wheat flour (or a mix of whole wheat and all-purpose flour)
- 1 cup self-rising flour
- 1/4 cup ground wattleseed (or substitute with ground roasted coffee for a similar flavor profile)
- 1/4 cup ground roasted wattleseed for topping (optional)
- 1 teaspoon salt
- 1 tablespoon honey or golden syrup
- 1 1/2 cups water (approximately)
- Olive oil, for greasing

Instructions:

1. Preheat the Oven:
    - Preheat your oven to 400°F (200°C). Place a baking stone or heavy baking sheet in the oven to heat.
2. Prepare the Dough:
    - In a large mixing bowl, combine the whole wheat flour, self-rising flour, ground wattleseed, and salt.
    - Add the honey or golden syrup to the dry ingredients.
    - Gradually add the water, mixing with a wooden spoon or your hands until a soft dough forms. You may need slightly more or less water, so add it gradually until you achieve the right consistency.
3. Shape the Bread:
    - Turn the dough out onto a lightly floured surface and knead it gently for a few minutes until smooth.
    - Shape the dough into a round loaf or oval shape, about 1 inch (2.5 cm) thick.
4. Bake the Bread:
    - Carefully remove the hot baking stone or baking sheet from the oven. Brush it lightly with olive oil.
    - Place the shaped bread dough onto the hot baking stone or baking sheet.
    - If desired, sprinkle the top of the bread with the ground roasted wattleseed for added flavor and decoration.
    - Bake in the preheated oven for 30-40 minutes, or until the bread is golden brown and sounds hollow when tapped on the bottom.

5. Cool and Serve:
    - Remove the bush bread from the oven and transfer it to a wire rack to cool completely.
    - Once cooled, slice and serve the bush bread with butter, honey, or your favorite toppings.

This bush bread is hearty, flavorful, and celebrates the use of native Australian ingredients. Enjoy it as a side dish, snack, or part of a bush tucker-inspired meal!

Lemon Meringue Pie

Ingredients:

For the crust:

- 1 1/4 cups all-purpose flour
- 1/2 cup (1 stick) unsalted butter, chilled and cut into small pieces
- 1/4 cup granulated sugar
- 1/4 teaspoon salt
- 3-4 tablespoons ice water

For the lemon filling:

- 1 cup granulated sugar
- 1/4 cup cornstarch
- 1/4 teaspoon salt
- 1 1/2 cups water
- 4 large egg yolks
- 1 tablespoon lemon zest
- 1/2 cup fresh lemon juice (about 3-4 lemons)
- 2 tablespoons unsalted butter

For the meringue:

- 4 large egg whites, at room temperature
- 1/4 teaspoon cream of tartar
- 1/2 cup granulated sugar
- 1/2 teaspoon vanilla extract

Instructions:

1. Prepare the crust:
    - In a food processor, combine the flour, sugar, and salt. Add the chilled butter pieces and pulse until the mixture resembles coarse crumbs.
    - Add the ice water, 1 tablespoon at a time, and pulse until the dough comes together.

- Shape the dough into a disk, wrap it in plastic wrap, and refrigerate for at least 30 minutes.
2. Preheat the oven:
    - Preheat your oven to 375°F (190°C).
3. Roll out the crust:
    - On a lightly floured surface, roll out the chilled dough into a circle about 12 inches in diameter. Transfer the dough to a 9-inch pie dish, pressing it gently into the bottom and sides. Trim any excess dough and crimp the edges. Prick the bottom of the crust with a fork.
    - Line the crust with parchment paper and fill it with pie weights or dried beans.
    - Bake in the preheated oven for 15 minutes. Remove the parchment paper and weights, and bake for an additional 5 minutes, or until the crust is golden brown. Set aside to cool.
4. Prepare the lemon filling:
    - In a medium saucepan, whisk together the sugar, cornstarch, and salt. Gradually whisk in the water until smooth.
    - Place the saucepan over medium heat and cook, stirring constantly, until the mixture thickens and comes to a boil.
    - Boil for 1 minute, then remove from heat.
    - In a separate bowl, whisk the egg yolks. Gradually whisk in about 1/2 cup of the hot sugar mixture to temper the eggs.
    - Gradually whisk the tempered egg mixture back into the saucepan. Return to heat and cook, stirring constantly, for another minute.
    - Remove from heat and stir in the lemon zest, lemon juice, and butter until smooth. Pour the filling into the cooled pie crust.
5. Prepare the meringue:
    - In a clean mixing bowl, beat the egg whites and cream of tartar with an electric mixer on medium speed until soft peaks form.
    - Gradually add the sugar, about 1 tablespoon at a time, while continuing to beat on high speed until stiff, glossy peaks form. Beat in the vanilla extract.
6. Top the pie with meringue:
    - Spread the meringue evenly over the hot lemon filling, making sure to spread it all the way to the edges of the crust to seal it.
    - Use the back of a spoon to create decorative peaks in the meringue.
7. Bake the pie:
    - Bake in the preheated oven for 10-12 minutes, or until the meringue is lightly golden brown.

8. Cool and serve:
    - Allow the pie to cool completely on a wire rack before slicing and serving. Refrigerate any leftovers.

Enjoy your homemade lemon meringue pie!

Lamington Cake

Ingredients:

For the cake:

- 2 cups all-purpose flour
- 1 cup granulated sugar
- 1/2 cup unsalted butter, softened
- 1 cup milk
- 2 teaspoons vanilla extract
- 2 teaspoons baking powder
- 1/4 teaspoon salt
- 4 large eggs

For the chocolate icing:

- 3 cups powdered sugar (icing sugar)
- 1/3 cup unsweetened cocoa powder
- 1/2 cup milk
- 2 tablespoons unsalted butter
- 1 teaspoon vanilla extract

For the coating:

- 3 cups desiccated coconut

Instructions:

1. Preheat the oven:
    - Preheat your oven to 350°F (175°C). Grease and flour a 9x13-inch cake pan or line it with parchment paper.
2. Make the cake:
    - In a large mixing bowl, cream together the softened butter and granulated sugar until light and fluffy.
    - Add the eggs, one at a time, beating well after each addition. Stir in the vanilla extract.
    - In a separate bowl, whisk together the flour, baking powder, and salt.

- Gradually add the dry ingredients to the wet ingredients, alternating with the milk, beginning and ending with the dry ingredients. Mix until just combined.
- Pour the batter into the prepared cake pan and spread it out evenly.
- Bake in the preheated oven for 25-30 minutes, or until a toothpick inserted into the center of the cake comes out clean.
- Remove the cake from the oven and let it cool completely in the pan.

3. Make the chocolate icing:
    - In a saucepan, combine the powdered sugar, cocoa powder, milk, butter, and vanilla extract.
    - Cook over medium heat, stirring constantly, until the mixture comes to a simmer and thickens slightly.
    - Remove from heat and let the icing cool slightly.

4. Assemble the Lamington cake:
    - Once the cake has cooled completely, remove it from the pan and cut it into squares or rectangles, depending on your preference.
    - Spread a layer of desiccated coconut on a shallow dish or baking sheet.
    - Dip each cake square into the chocolate icing, coating it completely.
    - Immediately roll the coated cake square in the desiccated coconut until evenly coated.
    - Place the coated cake squares on a wire rack to set.

5. Serve and enjoy:
    - Once the icing has set, transfer the Lamington cake squares to a serving platter.
    - Serve and enjoy these delicious homemade Lamington cakes with a cup of tea or coffee!

This Lamington cake recipe yields a delightful treat that combines fluffy cake with rich chocolate icing and coconut coating—a perfect dessert for any occasion!

Vanilla Bean Panna Cotta

Ingredients:

- 2 cups heavy cream
- 1/2 cup whole milk
- 1/2 cup granulated sugar
- 1 vanilla bean pod
- 2 1/4 teaspoons (1 packet) powdered gelatin
- 3 tablespoons cold water
- Fresh berries or fruit compote, for serving (optional)
- Mint leaves, for garnish (optional)

Instructions:

1. Prepare the Vanilla Bean:
    - Using a sharp knife, split the vanilla bean pod lengthwise, then scrape out the seeds using the back of the knife.
2. Infuse the Cream:
    - In a saucepan, combine the heavy cream, whole milk, granulated sugar, vanilla bean seeds, and the scraped vanilla bean pod.
    - Heat the mixture over medium heat, stirring occasionally, until it starts to steam. Do not let it boil.
    - Once steaming, remove the saucepan from the heat and let the mixture steep for about 15-20 minutes to infuse the flavors of the vanilla bean.
3. Bloom the Gelatin:
    - In a small bowl, sprinkle the powdered gelatin over the cold water and let it sit for about 5-10 minutes to bloom.
4. Strain the Cream Mixture:
    - After the cream mixture has steeped, remove the vanilla bean pod using a slotted spoon.
    - Strain the cream mixture through a fine-mesh sieve into a clean bowl to remove any remaining vanilla bean particles.
5. Combine the Cream and Gelatin:
    - Return the strained cream mixture to the saucepan and heat it over medium heat until it's warm but not boiling.
    - Add the bloomed gelatin to the warm cream mixture, stirring until the gelatin is completely dissolved.
6. Pour into Molds:

- Divide the cream mixture evenly among serving glasses or molds. You can use ramekins, small bowls, or silicone molds, depending on your preference.
- Refrigerate the panna cotta until set, typically for at least 4 hours or overnight.

7. Serve:
    - Once the panna cotta is set, you can serve it directly in the molds or unmold them onto serving plates by dipping the bottoms of the molds in hot water for a few seconds and then inverting them onto plates.
    - Serve the vanilla bean panna cotta chilled, either on its own or with fresh berries, fruit compote, or a drizzle of caramel sauce.
    - Garnish with mint leaves for a pop of color, if desired.

Enjoy the creamy and delicately flavored vanilla bean panna cotta as a refreshing and elegant dessert!

Chocolate Eclairs

Ingredients:

For the choux pastry:

- 1/2 cup (1 stick) unsalted butter
- 1 cup water
- 1 cup all-purpose flour
- 4 large eggs

For the pastry cream filling:

- 2 cups whole milk
- 1/2 cup granulated sugar
- 4 large egg yolks
- 1/4 cup cornstarch
- 1 teaspoon vanilla extract

For the chocolate icing:

- 1/2 cup heavy cream
- 4 ounces semisweet chocolate, chopped
- 1 tablespoon unsalted butter

Instructions:

1. Prepare the choux pastry:
    - Preheat your oven to 425°F (220°C). Line a baking sheet with parchment paper.
    - In a saucepan, combine the butter and water and bring to a boil over medium heat.
    - Remove the saucepan from the heat and quickly stir in the flour until a smooth dough forms.
    - Return the saucepan to low heat and cook the dough, stirring constantly, for 1-2 minutes to dry it out slightly.
    - Transfer the dough to a mixing bowl and let it cool for a few minutes.
    - Beat in the eggs, one at a time, mixing well after each addition, until the dough is smooth and glossy.
2. Pipe the pastry:

- Transfer the choux pastry dough to a pastry bag fitted with a large round tip.
- Pipe 4-inch long lines of dough onto the prepared baking sheet, leaving space between each eclair.
- Smooth down any peaks with a wet fingertip.
3. Bake the eclairs:
    - Place the baking sheet in the preheated oven and bake for 10 minutes.
    - Reduce the oven temperature to 375°F (190°C) and continue baking for an additional 20-25 minutes, or until the eclairs are golden brown and puffed.
    - Remove from the oven and let the eclairs cool completely on a wire rack.
4. Make the pastry cream filling:
    - In a saucepan, heat the milk over medium heat until it just begins to simmer.
    - In a mixing bowl, whisk together the sugar, egg yolks, and cornstarch until smooth.
    - Slowly pour the hot milk into the egg mixture, whisking constantly.
    - Return the mixture to the saucepan and cook over medium heat, whisking constantly, until thickened.
    - Remove from heat and stir in the vanilla extract.
    - Transfer the pastry cream to a bowl, cover with plastic wrap directly on the surface to prevent a skin from forming, and refrigerate until chilled.
5. Fill the eclairs:
    - Once the eclairs and pastry cream are cooled, use a sharp knife to make a small slit in the side of each eclair.
    - Transfer the pastry cream to a piping bag fitted with a small round tip.
    - Pipe the pastry cream into each eclair until filled.
6. Make the chocolate icing:
    - In a small saucepan, heat the heavy cream until it just begins to simmer.
    - Remove from heat and add the chopped chocolate and butter.
    - Let sit for 1-2 minutes, then stir until smooth and glossy.
7. Ice the eclairs:
    - Dip the top of each eclair into the chocolate icing, allowing any excess to drip off.
    - Place the chocolate-coated eclairs on a wire rack to set.
8. Serve and enjoy:
    - Once the chocolate icing is set, serve the chocolate eclairs immediately, or store them in the refrigerator until ready to serve.

These homemade chocolate eclairs are sure to impress with their crisp pastry shells, creamy filling, and decadent chocolate icing. Enjoy!

Caramel Slice (Millionaire's Shortbread)

Ingredients:

For the shortbread base:

- 1 cup (2 sticks) unsalted butter, softened
- 1/2 cup granulated sugar
- 2 cups all-purpose flour
- Pinch of salt

For the caramel filling:

- 1 can (14 ounces) sweetened condensed milk
- 1/2 cup (1 stick) unsalted butter
- 1/2 cup packed brown sugar
- 2 tablespoons golden syrup or light corn syrup
- 1 teaspoon vanilla extract

For the chocolate topping:

- 8 ounces semisweet chocolate, chopped
- 1 tablespoon unsalted butter

Instructions:

1. Preheat the oven: Preheat your oven to 350°F (175°C). Grease and line a 9x9-inch square baking pan with parchment paper, leaving an overhang on the sides for easy removal.
2. Make the shortbread base:
    - In a mixing bowl, cream together the softened butter and granulated sugar until light and fluffy.
    - Gradually add the flour and salt, mixing until a crumbly dough forms.
    - Press the dough evenly into the bottom of the prepared baking pan.
    - Bake in the preheated oven for 20-25 minutes, or until the shortbread is lightly golden. Remove from the oven and let it cool slightly.
3. Make the caramel filling:

- In a saucepan, combine the sweetened condensed milk, butter, brown sugar, and golden syrup.
- Cook over medium heat, stirring constantly, until the mixture comes to a gentle boil.
- Reduce the heat to low and continue cooking, stirring constantly, for 5-7 minutes, or until the caramel thickens and becomes golden brown.
- Remove from heat and stir in the vanilla extract.
- Pour the caramel evenly over the cooled shortbread base, then spread it out using a spatula. Allow it to cool completely.

4. Make the chocolate topping:
   - In a heatproof bowl set over a pot of simmering water (or in the microwave using short bursts of heat), melt the chopped chocolate and butter together until smooth and glossy.
   - Pour the melted chocolate over the cooled caramel layer, spreading it out evenly with a spatula.
5. Chill and set:
   - Place the caramel slice in the refrigerator for at least 2 hours, or until the chocolate is set.
6. Slice and serve:
   - Once set, use a sharp knife to cut the caramel slice into squares or bars.
   - Serve and enjoy!

This homemade caramel slice is rich, indulgent, and perfect for satisfying your sweet cravings. Store any leftovers in an airtight container in the refrigerator for up to 1 week. Enjoy!

Apple Crumble Pie

Ingredients:

For the crust:

- 1 1/4 cups all-purpose flour
- 1/2 teaspoon salt
- 1/2 cup (1 stick) unsalted butter, cold and cut into small cubes
- 2-4 tablespoons ice water

For the filling:

- 6 cups peeled, cored, and thinly sliced apples (such as Granny Smith or Honeycrisp)
- 1/2 cup granulated sugar
- 1/4 cup packed light brown sugar
- 2 tablespoons all-purpose flour
- 1 teaspoon ground cinnamon
- 1/4 teaspoon ground nutmeg
- 1 tablespoon lemon juice

For the crumble topping:

- 3/4 cup all-purpose flour
- 1/2 cup packed light brown sugar
- 1/2 cup old-fashioned rolled oats
- 1/2 teaspoon ground cinnamon
- 1/4 teaspoon salt
- 1/2 cup (1 stick) unsalted butter, melted

Instructions:

1. Prepare the crust:
    - In a large mixing bowl, whisk together the flour and salt. Add the cold cubed butter and use a pastry cutter or fork to cut the butter into the flour until the mixture resembles coarse crumbs.
    - Gradually add the ice water, 1 tablespoon at a time, and mix until the dough comes together and forms a ball.

- Flatten the dough into a disk, wrap it in plastic wrap, and refrigerate for at least 30 minutes.
2. Preheat the oven: Preheat your oven to 375°F (190°C). Place a baking sheet in the oven to preheat as well. This helps ensure a crispy bottom crust.
3. Prepare the filling:
    - In a large mixing bowl, combine the sliced apples, granulated sugar, brown sugar, flour, cinnamon, nutmeg, and lemon juice. Toss until the apples are evenly coated. Set aside.
4. Prepare the crumble topping:
    - In a separate bowl, combine the flour, brown sugar, rolled oats, cinnamon, and salt for the crumble topping.
    - Pour the melted butter over the dry ingredients and mix until the mixture resembles coarse crumbs. Set aside.
5. Assemble the pie:
    - On a lightly floured surface, roll out the chilled dough into a circle about 12 inches in diameter. Transfer the dough to a 9-inch pie dish, gently pressing it into the bottom and sides.
    - Trim any excess dough and crimp the edges as desired.
    - Pour the prepared apple filling into the pie crust, spreading it out evenly.
6. Add the crumble topping:
    - Sprinkle the crumble topping evenly over the apple filling, covering it completely.
7. Bake the pie:
    - Place the assembled pie on the preheated baking sheet in the oven. Bake for 45-55 minutes, or until the crust is golden brown and the filling is bubbly.
    - If the crumble topping starts to brown too quickly, cover the pie loosely with aluminum foil.
8. Cool and serve:
    - Remove the pie from the oven and let it cool on a wire rack for at least 1 hour before slicing.
    - Serve warm or at room temperature, optionally with a scoop of vanilla ice cream or a dollop of whipped cream.

Enjoy your homemade apple crumble pie, a perfect dessert for any occasion!

Wattleseed Brownies

Ingredients:

- 1/2 cup (1 stick) unsalted butter
- 8 ounces (about 1 1/3 cups) semisweet or bittersweet chocolate, chopped
- 1 cup granulated sugar
- 3 large eggs
- 1 teaspoon vanilla extract
- 1/2 cup all-purpose flour
- 2 tablespoons ground wattleseed
- 1/4 teaspoon salt
- Optional: Chopped nuts, such as macadamia nuts or walnuts (about 1/2 cup)

Instructions:

1. Preheat the oven: Preheat your oven to 350°F (175°C). Grease and line an 8x8-inch baking pan with parchment paper, leaving an overhang on the sides for easy removal.
2. Melt the butter and chocolate: In a heatproof bowl set over a pot of simmering water (or in the microwave using short bursts of heat), melt the butter and chopped chocolate together until smooth and well combined. Remove from heat and let cool slightly.
3. Prepare the batter: In a mixing bowl, whisk together the granulated sugar, eggs, and vanilla extract until well combined. Slowly pour the melted chocolate mixture into the egg mixture, stirring constantly until smooth.
4. Add the dry ingredients: In a separate bowl, whisk together the all-purpose flour, ground wattleseed, and salt. Gradually add the dry ingredients to the wet ingredients, stirring until just combined. Be careful not to overmix. If using chopped nuts, fold them into the batter at this stage.
5. Bake the brownies: Pour the batter into the prepared baking pan and spread it out evenly with a spatula. Tap the pan gently on the counter to release any air bubbles. Bake in the preheated oven for 25-30 minutes, or until the top is set and a toothpick inserted into the center comes out with a few moist crumbs.
6. Cool and slice: Remove the brownies from the oven and let them cool completely in the pan on a wire rack. Once cooled, use the parchment paper overhang to lift the brownies out of the pan and transfer them to a cutting board. Slice into squares or bars.

7. Serve and enjoy: Serve the wattleseed brownies at room temperature, optionally dusted with powdered sugar or drizzled with melted chocolate for extra decadence. Enjoy the unique flavor and rich texture of these delicious brownies!

These wattleseed brownies are perfect for sharing with friends and family or enjoying as a special treat for yourself. Enjoy the wonderful combination of chocolate and wattleseed flavors in every bite!

Lemon Delicious Pudding

Ingredients:

- 4 large eggs, separated
- 1 cup granulated sugar
- 1/3 cup all-purpose flour
- Zest of 2 lemons
- 1/2 cup fresh lemon juice (about 3-4 lemons)
- 1 1/2 cups milk
- Confectioners' sugar, for dusting (optional)
- Whipped cream or vanilla ice cream, for serving (optional)

Instructions:

1. Preheat the oven: Preheat your oven to 350°F (175°C). Butter a 2-quart baking dish or individual ramekins and place them in a larger baking dish.
2. Separate the eggs: Separate the egg whites and yolks into two large mixing bowls.
3. Beat the egg yolks with sugar: In the bowl with the egg yolks, add the granulated sugar and beat until pale and creamy.
4. Add lemon zest and juice: Stir in the lemon zest and lemon juice until well combined.
5. Add flour and milk: Gradually add the flour and milk to the egg yolk mixture, alternating between the two, and stirring until smooth.
6. Beat the egg whites: In the other bowl with the egg whites, beat them until stiff peaks form.
7. Fold egg whites into the mixture: Gently fold the beaten egg whites into the lemon mixture until just combined. Be careful not to deflate the egg whites too much.
8. Pour into baking dish: Pour the mixture into the prepared baking dish or ramekins.
9. Create a water bath: Place the larger baking dish with the filled ramekins in the preheated oven. Carefully pour hot water into the larger baking dish until it reaches halfway up the sides of the ramekins. This creates a water bath, which helps the pudding cook evenly.
10. Bake: Bake for 30-35 minutes, or until the top is golden brown and set, and a skewer inserted into the center comes out mostly clean. The pudding will have a sponge-like texture on top with a lemon sauce underneath.

11. Serve: Remove the pudding from the oven and let it cool for a few minutes. Dust with confectioners' sugar if desired and serve warm with whipped cream or vanilla ice cream.

Enjoy the delightful tangy and comforting flavor of this classic Lemon Delicious Pudding!

Vanilla Sponge Cake with Passionfruit Icing

Ingredients:

For the Vanilla Sponge Cake:

- 1 and 1/2 cups all-purpose flour
- 1 and 1/2 teaspoons baking powder
- 1/4 teaspoon salt
- 1/2 cup unsalted butter, softened
- 1 cup granulated sugar
- 3 large eggs
- 1 teaspoon vanilla extract
- 1/2 cup milk

For the Passionfruit Icing:

- 1 cup powdered sugar (confectioners' sugar)
- 2-3 tablespoons passionfruit pulp (strained if desired)
- 1-2 tablespoons lemon juice
- Additional passionfruit pulp for drizzling (optional)

Instructions:

1. Preheat the oven: Preheat your oven to 350°F (175°C). Grease and flour a 9-inch round cake pan or line it with parchment paper.
2. Make the vanilla sponge cake:
    - In a medium bowl, sift together the all-purpose flour, baking powder, and salt. Set aside.
    - In a large mixing bowl, cream together the softened butter and granulated sugar until light and fluffy.
    - Beat in the eggs, one at a time, until well combined. Stir in the vanilla extract.
    - Gradually add the dry ingredients to the wet ingredients, alternating with the milk, beginning and ending with the dry ingredients. Mix until just combined, being careful not to overmix.

- Pour the batter into the prepared cake pan and spread it out evenly with a spatula.
- Bake in the preheated oven for 25-30 minutes, or until a toothpick inserted into the center of the cake comes out clean.
- Remove the cake from the oven and let it cool in the pan for 10 minutes before transferring it to a wire rack to cool completely.

3. Make the passionfruit icing:
    - In a small bowl, whisk together the powdered sugar, passionfruit pulp, and lemon juice until smooth. Adjust the consistency by adding more powdered sugar or lemon juice as needed.
    - Once the cake has cooled completely, spread the passionfruit icing evenly over the top of the cake.
    - If desired, drizzle additional passionfruit pulp over the icing for extra flavor and decoration.
4. Serve and enjoy:
    - Slice the vanilla sponge cake with passionfruit icing into wedges and serve.
    - Store any leftovers in an airtight container at room temperature for up to 3 days.

This Vanilla Sponge Cake with Passionfruit Icing is perfect for any occasion, from afternoon tea to special celebrations. Enjoy the combination of light, fluffy cake with tangy and tropical passionfruit flavor!

Anzac Cake

Ingredients:

For the cake:

- 1 cup rolled oats
- 1 cup desiccated coconut
- 1 cup all-purpose flour
- 1 cup granulated sugar
- 1/2 cup unsalted butter, melted
- 2 tablespoons golden syrup
- 1 teaspoon baking soda
- 1 cup boiling water

For the icing:

- 1 cup powdered sugar (confectioners' sugar)
- 2 tablespoons cocoa powder
- 2 tablespoons boiling water
- 1 tablespoon unsalted butter, melted
- Shredded coconut, for garnish (optional)

Instructions:

1. Preheat the oven: Preheat your oven to 350°F (175°C). Grease and line a 9-inch square baking pan with parchment paper, leaving an overhang on the sides for easy removal.
2. Make the cake batter:
    - In a large mixing bowl, combine the rolled oats, desiccated coconut, all-purpose flour, and granulated sugar.
    - In a small saucepan, melt the unsalted butter and golden syrup together over low heat.
    - In a small bowl, dissolve the baking soda in the boiling water, then add it to the melted butter and golden syrup mixture. Stir to combine.
    - Pour the wet mixture over the dry ingredients and mix until well combined.
3. Bake the cake:
    - Pour the cake batter into the prepared baking pan and spread it out evenly.

- Bake in the preheated oven for 30-35 minutes, or until a toothpick inserted into the center of the cake comes out clean.
- Remove the cake from the oven and let it cool completely in the pan.
4. Make the icing:
    - In a small bowl, sift together the powdered sugar and cocoa powder.
    - Add the boiling water and melted butter to the powdered sugar mixture and stir until smooth and well combined.
5. Ice the cake:
    - Once the cake has cooled completely, spread the icing evenly over the top of the cake.
    - Sprinkle shredded coconut over the icing for garnish, if desired.
6. Slice and serve:
    - Use the parchment paper overhang to lift the cake out of the pan and transfer it to a cutting board.
    - Slice the Anzac Cake into squares or bars and serve.

Enjoy this delicious Anzac Cake as a sweet treat with the distinctive flavors of oats, coconut, and golden syrup, perfect for sharing with friends and family!

Chocolate Lamingtons

Ingredients:

For the sponge cake:

- 1 1/2 cups all-purpose flour
- 2 teaspoons baking powder
- 1/4 teaspoon salt
- 1/2 cup unsalted butter, softened
- 3/4 cup granulated sugar
- 2 large eggs
- 1 teaspoon vanilla extract
- 1/2 cup milk

For the chocolate icing:

- 3 cups powdered sugar (confectioners' sugar)
- 1/4 cup unsweetened cocoa powder
- 2 tablespoons unsalted butter, melted
- 1/2 cup milk
- 2 cups desiccated coconut, for rolling

Instructions:

1. Preheat the oven: Preheat your oven to 350°F (175°C). Grease and flour a 9x13-inch baking pan or line it with parchment paper.
2. Make the sponge cake:
    - In a medium bowl, sift together the all-purpose flour, baking powder, and salt. Set aside.
    - In a large mixing bowl, cream together the softened butter and granulated sugar until light and fluffy.
    - Add the eggs one at a time, beating well after each addition. Stir in the vanilla extract.
    - Gradually add the dry ingredients to the wet ingredients, alternating with the milk, and mix until smooth and well combined.
    - Pour the batter into the prepared baking pan and spread it out evenly.

- Bake in the preheated oven for 25-30 minutes, or until a toothpick inserted into the center comes out clean.
- Remove the cake from the oven and let it cool completely in the pan.
3. Cut the cake into squares:
    - Once the cake has cooled, transfer it to a cutting board and cut it into 2-inch squares.
4. Prepare the chocolate icing:
    - In a medium bowl, sift together the powdered sugar and cocoa powder.
    - Add the melted butter and milk to the powdered sugar mixture and whisk until smooth and well combined.
5. Coat the cake squares:
    - Place the desiccated coconut in a shallow bowl.
    - Dip each cake square into the chocolate icing, ensuring it is completely coated.
    - Allow any excess icing to drip off, then roll the coated cake square in the desiccated coconut until fully covered.
    - Place the coated Lamingtons on a wire rack to set.
6. Serve and enjoy:
    - Once the chocolate icing has set, transfer the Chocolate Lamingtons to a serving platter.
    - Serve and enjoy these delicious Australian treats with a cup of tea or coffee!

These Chocolate Lamingtons are perfect for afternoon tea, parties, or as a special treat any time of the day. Enjoy their rich chocolatey flavor and delightful texture!

Date and Walnut Scones

Ingredients:

- 2 cups all-purpose flour
- 1/4 cup granulated sugar
- 1 tablespoon baking powder
- 1/2 teaspoon salt
- 1/2 cup unsalted butter, cold and cut into small cubes
- 1/2 cup chopped dates
- 1/2 cup chopped walnuts
- 2/3 cup milk
- 1 teaspoon vanilla extract
- Optional: Additional milk for brushing
- Optional: Granulated sugar for sprinkling

Instructions:

1. Preheat the oven: Preheat your oven to 400°F (200°C). Line a baking sheet with parchment paper or lightly grease it.
2. Prepare the dry ingredients:
    - In a large mixing bowl, whisk together the all-purpose flour, granulated sugar, baking powder, and salt until well combined.
3. Incorporate the butter:
    - Add the cold, cubed butter to the dry ingredients. Use a pastry cutter or your fingertips to rub the butter into the flour mixture until it resembles coarse crumbs.
4. Add the dates and walnuts:
    - Stir in the chopped dates and chopped walnuts until evenly distributed throughout the mixture.
5. Combine wet ingredients:
    - In a separate small bowl, whisk together the milk and vanilla extract.
6. Form the dough:
    - Gradually add the milk mixture to the dry ingredients, stirring until a dough forms. Be careful not to overmix.
7. Shape the scones:
    - Transfer the dough onto a lightly floured surface. Gently pat the dough into a circle or rectangle, about 1 inch (2.5 cm) thick.

- Use a floured biscuit cutter or knife to cut out scones from the dough. Place the scones onto the prepared baking sheet, leaving some space between each scone.
8. Bake the scones:
    - Optional: Brush the tops of the scones with a little milk and sprinkle with granulated sugar for extra shine and sweetness.
    - Bake in the preheated oven for 12-15 minutes, or until the scones are golden brown and cooked through.
9. Serve and enjoy:
    - Once baked, transfer the scones to a wire rack to cool slightly.
    - Serve warm with butter, clotted cream, or your favorite jam.

These date and walnut scones are perfect for breakfast, brunch, or afternoon tea. Enjoy their delicious flavor and tender texture!

Caramel Banana Tart

Ingredients:

For the tart crust:

- 1 1/4 cups all-purpose flour
- 1/4 cup granulated sugar
- 1/2 cup unsalted butter, cold and cubed
- 1 large egg yolk
- 2 tablespoons ice water

For the caramel filling:

- 1 cup granulated sugar
- 1/4 cup water
- 1/2 cup heavy cream
- 2 tablespoons unsalted butter
- Pinch of salt

For assembling:

- 3-4 ripe bananas, sliced

Instructions:

1. Prepare the Tart Crust:
    - In a food processor, pulse together the flour and sugar. Add the cold cubed butter and pulse until the mixture resembles coarse crumbs.
    - Add the egg yolk and ice water, and pulse until the dough comes together.
    - Turn the dough out onto a lightly floured surface and knead it gently until smooth. Shape it into a disk, wrap in plastic wrap, and refrigerate for at least 30 minutes.
2. Preheat the Oven:
    - Preheat your oven to 375°F (190°C).
3. Roll out the Dough:
    - On a floured surface, roll out the chilled dough into a circle about 12 inches in diameter. Transfer it to a tart pan and press it gently into the bottom and sides. Trim any excess dough.
4. Blind Bake the Crust:

- Line the tart shell with parchment paper and fill it with pie weights or dried beans.
- Bake the crust for about 15 minutes, then remove the parchment paper and weights. Continue baking for another 10-15 minutes, or until the crust is golden brown. Remove from the oven and let it cool completely.

5. Prepare the Caramel Filling:
   - In a saucepan, combine the granulated sugar and water. Cook over medium heat, swirling the pan occasionally, until the sugar dissolves and the mixture turns a deep amber color.
   - Remove the saucepan from the heat and carefully add the heavy cream, butter, and salt. Be cautious as the mixture will bubble up.
   - Return the saucepan to low heat and cook, stirring constantly, until the caramel is smooth. Remove from heat and let it cool slightly.
6. Assemble the Tart:
   - Pour the caramel filling into the cooled tart shell.
   - Arrange the sliced bananas on top of the caramel in a decorative pattern.
7. Chill and Serve:
   - Refrigerate the tart for at least 1 hour to set the caramel.
   - Serve chilled, optionally garnished with whipped cream or a sprinkle of powdered sugar.

Enjoy your indulgent caramel banana tart!

Apricot Jam Drops

Ingredients:

- 1/2 cup unsalted butter, softened
- 1/3 cup granulated sugar
- 1 teaspoon vanilla extract
- 1 egg
- 1 1/4 cups all-purpose flour
- 1/4 teaspoon baking powder
- Pinch of salt
- Apricot jam (or any other jam of your choice)

Instructions:

1. Preheat the Oven:
    - Preheat your oven to 350°F (175°C). Line a baking sheet with parchment paper.
2. Cream the Butter and Sugar:
    - In a mixing bowl, cream together the softened butter and granulated sugar until light and fluffy.
3. Add Vanilla and Egg:
    - Beat in the vanilla extract and egg until well combined.
4. Combine Dry Ingredients:
    - In a separate bowl, sift together the all-purpose flour, baking powder, and salt.
5. Mix the Dough:
    - Gradually add the dry ingredients to the butter mixture, mixing until a soft dough forms.
6. Form Dough Balls:
    - Roll the dough into small balls, about 1 inch in diameter, and place them on the prepared baking sheet, leaving space between each ball.
7. Make Indentations:
    - Use your thumb or the back of a spoon to gently press an indentation into the center of each dough ball.
8. Fill with Jam:
    - Spoon a small amount of apricot jam (or your preferred jam) into each indentation, filling it almost to the top.

9. Bake:
    - Bake the jam drops in the preheated oven for 10-12 minutes, or until the edges are lightly golden.
10. Cool and Serve:
    - Allow the jam drops to cool on the baking sheet for a few minutes before transferring them to a wire rack to cool completely.

These apricot jam drops are best enjoyed once they have cooled slightly but are still warm and the jam is slightly gooey. They'll be a hit with anyone who loves a fruity, buttery treat!

Lemonade Scones

Ingredients:

- 2 cups self-rising flour
- 1/4 cup granulated sugar
- 1/2 cup heavy cream
- 1/2 cup lemonade (carbonated)
- Zest of 1 lemon (optional, for extra lemon flavor)
- Additional heavy cream, for brushing (optional)
- Additional granulated sugar, for sprinkling (optional)

Instructions:

1. Preheat the Oven:
    - Preheat your oven to 425°F (220°C). Line a baking sheet with parchment paper.
2. Prepare the Dough:
    - In a large mixing bowl, sift together the self-rising flour and granulated sugar. If you're using lemon zest, add it to the bowl as well and mix to combine.
    - Make a well in the center of the dry ingredients.
3. Add Wet Ingredients:
    - Pour the heavy cream and lemonade into the well in the dry ingredients.
4. Mix the Dough:
    - Using a wooden spoon or spatula, gently mix the wet and dry ingredients together until a soft dough forms. Be careful not to overmix.
5. Shape the Scones:
    - Turn the dough out onto a lightly floured surface and gently pat it into a circle about 1 inch thick.
6. Cut the Scones:
    - Use a floured round cutter (about 2 inches in diameter) to cut out scones from the dough. Place the scones onto the prepared baking sheet, leaving a little space between each one.
7. Bake:
    - Brush the tops of the scones with a little extra heavy cream, if desired, and sprinkle with granulated sugar for a sweet, crunchy crust.

- Bake in the preheated oven for 10-12 minutes, or until the scones are lightly golden brown on top and cooked through.
8. Cool and Serve:
    - Transfer the scones to a wire rack to cool slightly before serving. Enjoy them warm with a dollop of clotted cream and your favorite jam.

These lemonade scones are light, fluffy, and subtly sweet with a hint of lemon flavor.

They're perfect for a quick and easy treat, whether you're enjoying them for breakfast, brunch, or afternoon tea!

Chocolate Custard Tart

Ingredients:

For the tart crust:

- 1 1/4 cups all-purpose flour
- 1/4 cup granulated sugar
- 1/2 cup unsalted butter, cold and cubed
- 1 large egg yolk
- 2 tablespoons ice water

For the chocolate custard filling:

- 2 cups whole milk
- 1/2 cup granulated sugar
- 1/4 cup unsweetened cocoa powder
- 4 large egg yolks
- 1/4 cup cornstarch
- 1 teaspoon vanilla extract
- 4 ounces bittersweet chocolate, chopped

Instructions:

1. Prepare the Tart Crust:
    - In a food processor, pulse together the flour and sugar. Add the cold cubed butter and pulse until the mixture resembles coarse crumbs.
    - Add the egg yolk and ice water, and pulse until the dough comes together.
    - Turn the dough out onto a lightly floured surface and knead it gently until smooth. Shape it into a disk, wrap in plastic wrap, and refrigerate for at least 30 minutes.
2. Preheat the Oven:
    - Preheat your oven to 375°F (190°C).
3. Roll out the Dough:
    - On a floured surface, roll out the chilled dough into a circle about 12 inches in diameter. Transfer it to a 9-inch tart pan and press it gently into the bottom and sides. Trim any excess dough.
4. Blind Bake the Crust:

- Line the tart shell with parchment paper and fill it with pie weights or dried beans.
- Bake the crust for about 15 minutes, then remove the parchment paper and weights. Continue baking for another 10-15 minutes, or until the crust is golden brown. Remove from the oven and let it cool slightly.

5. Prepare the Chocolate Custard Filling:
   - In a saucepan, heat the whole milk over medium heat until it just begins to simmer.
   - In a separate bowl, whisk together the granulated sugar, cocoa powder, egg yolks, and cornstarch until smooth.
   - Gradually pour the hot milk into the egg mixture, whisking constantly, until well combined.
   - Return the mixture to the saucepan and cook over medium heat, stirring constantly, until it thickens and coats the back of a spoon.
   - Remove from heat and stir in the vanilla extract and chopped bittersweet chocolate until the chocolate is melted and the mixture is smooth.

6. Assemble and Bake the Tart:
   - Pour the chocolate custard filling into the cooled tart shell and spread it out evenly.
   - Bake the tart in the preheated oven for 15-20 minutes, or until the custard is set around the edges but slightly jiggly in the center.
   - Remove from the oven and let it cool completely on a wire rack.

7. Chill and Serve:
   - Once cooled, refrigerate the tart for at least 2 hours, or until the custard is fully set.
   - Serve chilled, optionally garnished with whipped cream or chocolate shavings.

Enjoy your delicious chocolate custard tart! It's sure to be a hit with chocolate lovers everywhere.

Vanilla Wattleseed Macarons

Ingredients:

For the macaron shells:

- 1 cup almond flour
- 1 3/4 cups powdered sugar
- 3 large egg whites, room temperature
- 1/4 cup granulated sugar
- 1 teaspoon vanilla extract
- 1 tablespoon wattleseed powder

For the vanilla wattleseed buttercream filling:

- 1/2 cup unsalted butter, softened
- 1 1/2 cups powdered sugar
- 1 teaspoon vanilla extract
- 1 tablespoon wattleseed powder

Instructions:

1. Prepare the Macaron Shells:
    - Line two baking sheets with parchment paper.
    - In a large bowl, sift together the almond flour, powdered sugar, and wattleseed powder. Set aside.
    - In a separate bowl, beat the egg whites with an electric mixer until foamy. Gradually add the granulated sugar while continuing to beat, until stiff, glossy peaks form.
    - Add the vanilla extract to the egg whites and gently fold it in.
    - Gradually add the sifted almond flour mixture to the egg whites, folding gently until the batter is smooth and shiny. Be careful not to overmix.
    - Transfer the batter to a piping bag fitted with a round tip.
    - Pipe small circles of batter onto the prepared baking sheets, spacing them about 1 inch apart.
    - Let the piped macarons sit at room temperature for about 30-60 minutes, until a skin forms on the surface and they are no longer sticky to the touch.
2. Bake the Macarons:

- Preheat your oven to 300°F (150°C).
- Bake the macarons in the preheated oven for 15-18 minutes, rotating the baking sheets halfway through, until the macarons are set and have developed feet.
- Remove the macarons from the oven and let them cool completely on the baking sheets before removing them.
3. Prepare the Vanilla Wattleseed Buttercream Filling:
    - In a mixing bowl, beat the softened butter until creamy.
    - Gradually add the powdered sugar, vanilla extract, and wattleseed powder, and beat until smooth and well combined. Adjust the consistency by adding more powdered sugar if needed.
4. Assemble the Macarons:
    - Pair the cooled macaron shells based on similar sizes.
    - Transfer the vanilla wattleseed buttercream filling into a piping bag fitted with a round tip.
    - Pipe a small amount of filling onto the flat side of one macaron shell and sandwich it with another shell, gently pressing down to spread the filling to the edges.
    - Repeat with the remaining macaron shells and filling.
5. Chill and Serve:
    - Place the assembled macarons in an airtight container and refrigerate them for at least 24 hours to allow the flavors to meld and the texture to set.
    - Serve chilled and enjoy your delicious vanilla wattleseed macarons!

These macarons are sure to impress with their unique flavor combination and delicate texture. They make a wonderful treat for special occasions or any time you're craving something sweet and sophisticated.

Cherry Ripe Slice

Ingredients:

For the base:

- 200g (about 7 oz) sweet biscuits (such as Graham crackers or Digestive biscuits)
- 1 cup desiccated coconut
- 1/4 cup cocoa powder
- 100g (about 3.5 oz) unsalted butter, melted

For the filling:

- 395g (about 14 oz) sweetened condensed milk
- 1 cup desiccated coconut
- 1 cup glace cherries, chopped
- 1 teaspoon vanilla extract

For the topping:

- 200g (about 7 oz) dark chocolate, chopped
- 1 tablespoon vegetable oil
- Additional desiccated coconut, for sprinkling (optional)

Instructions:

1. Prepare the Base:
    - Line a 9x9 inch square baking pan with parchment paper, leaving some overhang for easy removal later.
    - Crush the sweet biscuits into fine crumbs. You can do this by placing them in a food processor or placing them in a sealed plastic bag and crushing them with a rolling pin.
    - In a mixing bowl, combine the crushed biscuits, desiccated coconut, cocoa powder, and melted butter. Mix until well combined.
    - Press the mixture firmly and evenly into the bottom of the prepared baking pan. Use the back of a spoon or a flat-bottomed glass to compact the mixture.

- Place the pan in the refrigerator to chill while you prepare the filling.
2. Prepare the Filling:
    - In a mixing bowl, combine the sweetened condensed milk, desiccated coconut, chopped glace cherries, and vanilla extract. Stir until evenly mixed.
    - Spread the filling evenly over the chilled biscuit base in the baking pan, smoothing the top with a spatula or the back of a spoon.
    - Return the pan to the refrigerator while you prepare the topping.
3. Prepare the Topping:
    - In a heatproof bowl set over a pot of simmering water (or in the microwave using short bursts of heat), melt the chopped dark chocolate and vegetable oil together, stirring until smooth.
    - Pour the melted chocolate over the chilled filling layer in the baking pan, spreading it evenly with a spatula to cover the entire surface.
    - Optional: Sprinkle some additional desiccated coconut over the melted chocolate for decoration.
4. Chill and Serve:
    - Return the pan to the refrigerator and chill the Cherry Ripe slice for at least 2-3 hours, or until the chocolate topping is set.
    - Once set, use the parchment paper overhang to lift the slice out of the pan and transfer it to a cutting board.
    - Use a sharp knife to cut the slice into squares or bars.
    - Serve chilled and enjoy!

This Cherry Ripe slice is a heavenly combination of chocolate, cherries, and coconut that's perfect for satisfying your sweet cravings. It's great for sharing at parties or as a special treat for yourself and your loved ones.

Butterscotch Pudding

Ingredients:

- 1/2 cup (1 stick) unsalted butter
- 1 cup packed brown sugar
- 1/4 cup cornstarch
- 1/2 teaspoon salt
- 4 cups whole milk
- 4 large egg yolks
- 2 teaspoons vanilla extract
- Whipped cream, for serving (optional)

Instructions:

1. Melt the Butter:
    - In a medium saucepan, melt the butter over medium heat.
2. Make the Butterscotch Sauce:
    - Once the butter is melted, add the packed brown sugar to the saucepan. Stir constantly until the sugar has dissolved and the mixture is smooth and bubbly, about 2-3 minutes.
3. Mix the Cornstarch Slurry:
    - In a small bowl, whisk together the cornstarch and salt. Gradually whisk in about 1/2 cup of the milk until smooth and no lumps remain.
4. Combine Ingredients:
    - Slowly pour the remaining milk into the saucepan with the butterscotch mixture, stirring constantly.
    - Whisk in the cornstarch slurry until well combined.
5. Cook the Pudding:
    - Bring the mixture to a gentle boil over medium heat, stirring constantly. Once it begins to boil, reduce the heat to low and simmer for 2-3 minutes, stirring continuously, until the pudding has thickened.
6. Temper the Egg Yolks:
    - In a separate bowl, whisk the egg yolks. Slowly pour about 1 cup of the hot pudding mixture into the egg yolks, whisking constantly to temper them.
7. Add Egg Yolks to Pudding:
    - Pour the tempered egg yolk mixture back into the saucepan with the remaining pudding mixture, whisking constantly to combine.

8. Cook Until Thickened:
    - Cook the pudding for an additional 2-3 minutes over low heat, stirring continuously, until it has thickened to a pudding-like consistency.
9. Remove from Heat and Add Vanilla:
    - Remove the saucepan from the heat and stir in the vanilla extract until well incorporated.
10. Chill:
    - Pour the butterscotch pudding into individual serving dishes or a large bowl.
    - Cover the surface of the pudding with plastic wrap to prevent a skin from forming.
    - Refrigerate for at least 2-3 hours, or until the pudding is chilled and set.
11. Serve:
    - Serve the butterscotch pudding chilled, topped with whipped cream if desired.

Enjoy the creamy, caramelized goodness of homemade butterscotch pudding!

Coffee Scroll

Ingredients:

For the dough:

- 3 cups all-purpose flour
- 1/4 cup granulated sugar
- 2 1/4 teaspoons (1 packet) instant yeast
- 1/2 teaspoon salt
- 1/2 cup unsalted butter, melted
- 1/2 cup warm milk (about 110°F or 45°C)
- 2 large eggs

For the coffee filling:

- 1/2 cup granulated sugar
- 2 tablespoons instant coffee granules
- 1 tablespoon unsweetened cocoa powder
- 1/4 cup unsalted butter, softened

For the glaze (optional):

- 1 cup powdered sugar
- 1-2 tablespoons brewed coffee
- 1/2 teaspoon vanilla extract

Instructions:

1. Prepare the Dough:
    - In a large mixing bowl, combine the flour, sugar, instant yeast, and salt.
    - In a separate bowl, whisk together the melted butter, warm milk, and eggs.
    - Pour the wet ingredients into the dry ingredients and mix until a dough forms.
    - Turn the dough out onto a lightly floured surface and knead for about 5-7 minutes, or until the dough is smooth and elastic.

- Place the dough in a greased bowl, cover with a clean kitchen towel, and let it rise in a warm place for about 1 hour, or until doubled in size.
2. Make the Coffee Filling:
    - In a small bowl, mix together the granulated sugar, instant coffee granules, and cocoa powder until well combined.
    - Stir in the softened butter until a thick, spreadable mixture forms.
3. Assemble the Scrolls:
    - Punch down the risen dough and roll it out on a lightly floured surface into a large rectangle, about 12x18 inches.
    - Spread the coffee filling evenly over the surface of the dough, leaving a small border around the edges.
    - Starting from one long side, tightly roll up the dough into a log. Pinch the seam to seal.
4. Slice and Arrange:
    - Using a sharp knife or a piece of unflavored dental floss, slice the dough log into 12 equal pieces.
    - Place the slices in a greased 9x13-inch baking dish, leaving a little space between each one.
5. Second Rise:
    - Cover the baking dish with a clean kitchen towel and let the scrolls rise for another 30-45 minutes, or until puffy and slightly expanded.
6. Bake:
    - Preheat your oven to 350°F (175°C).
    - Once the scrolls have risen, bake them in the preheated oven for 20-25 minutes, or until golden brown and cooked through.
    - Remove from the oven and let them cool slightly in the pan.
7. Make the Glaze (Optional):
    - In a small bowl, whisk together the powdered sugar, brewed coffee, and vanilla extract until smooth. Adjust the consistency by adding more coffee or powdered sugar as needed.
8. Glaze and Serve:
    - Drizzle the glaze over the warm coffee scrolls.
    - Serve the scrolls warm or at room temperature, and enjoy with a cup of coffee or tea!

These coffee scrolls are perfect for breakfast, brunch, or as a sweet treat any time of day. The combination of the rich coffee filling and sweet dough is sure to be a hit!

Coconut Ice

Ingredients:

- 3 cups powdered sugar (also known as icing sugar)
- 3 cups desiccated coconut
- 1 can (14 ounces) sweetened condensed milk
- 1 teaspoon vanilla extract
- Pink food coloring (optional)

Instructions:

1. Prepare the Pan:
    - Line an 8x8 inch square baking dish with parchment paper, leaving some overhang on the sides for easy removal. This will make it easier to lift the coconut ice out of the pan later.
2. Mix the Dry Ingredients:
    - In a large mixing bowl, sift the powdered sugar to remove any lumps.
    - Add the desiccated coconut to the powdered sugar and mix until well combined.
3. Add the Wet Ingredients:
    - Pour the sweetened condensed milk and vanilla extract over the dry ingredients.
4. Mix the Dough:
    - Using a spatula or wooden spoon, mix the ingredients together until a thick, sticky dough forms. Make sure all the dry ingredients are well incorporated into the condensed milk.
5. Divide the Dough:
    - Divide the dough in half. Leave one half plain and transfer it to the prepared baking dish, pressing it down firmly and evenly into the bottom of the pan.
6. Color the Remaining Dough (Optional):
    - If desired, add a few drops of pink food coloring to the remaining dough in the mixing bowl. Mix until the color is evenly distributed and the dough is uniformly pink.
7. Layer the Dough:
    - Carefully spread the pink dough over the plain dough in the baking dish, pressing it down gently and evenly to create a smooth surface.

8. Chill:
    - Place the baking dish in the refrigerator and chill the coconut ice for at least 2-3 hours, or until firm and set.
9. Slice and Serve:
    - Once the coconut ice is completely chilled and set, use the parchment paper overhang to lift it out of the pan.
    - Place it on a cutting board and use a sharp knife to cut it into squares or bars.
    - Serve the coconut ice immediately, or store it in an airtight container in the refrigerator for up to a week.

Enjoy the sweet and coconutty goodness of homemade coconut ice! It's a delightful treat for any occasion, whether you're enjoying it as a snack, dessert, or homemade gift.

Custard-filled Profiteroles

Ingredients:

For the choux pastry:

- 1/2 cup water
- 1/2 cup whole milk
- 1/2 cup unsalted butter, cut into small pieces
- 1 tablespoon granulated sugar
- 1/4 teaspoon salt
- 1 cup all-purpose flour
- 4 large eggs, at room temperature

For the custard filling:

- 2 cups whole milk
- 1/2 cup granulated sugar
- 1/4 cup cornstarch
- 4 large egg yolks
- 1 teaspoon vanilla extract

For the chocolate sauce (optional):

- 4 ounces semisweet chocolate, chopped
- 1/2 cup heavy cream
- 2 tablespoons unsalted butter

Instructions:

1. Make the Choux Pastry:
    - Preheat your oven to 400°F (200°C). Line a baking sheet with parchment paper.
    - In a medium saucepan, combine the water, milk, butter, sugar, and salt. Heat over medium heat until the mixture comes to a boil and the butter is melted.

- Add the flour all at once and stir vigorously with a wooden spoon until the mixture forms a ball and pulls away from the sides of the pan.
- Transfer the mixture to a mixing bowl and let it cool for a few minutes.
- Add the eggs, one at a time, beating well after each addition until the dough is smooth and glossy.

2. Pipe the Pastry:
   - Transfer the choux pastry dough to a piping bag fitted with a large round tip.
   - Pipe small mounds of dough onto the prepared baking sheet, leaving some space between each one.
3. Bake the Profiteroles:
   - Bake the profiteroles in the preheated oven for 20-25 minutes, or until they are puffed up and golden brown.
   - Remove them from the oven and transfer to a wire rack to cool completely.
4. Make the Custard Filling:
   - In a saucepan, heat the milk over medium heat until it just begins to simmer.
   - In a separate bowl, whisk together the granulated sugar, cornstarch, and egg yolks until smooth and well combined.
   - Gradually pour the hot milk into the egg mixture, whisking constantly.
   - Return the mixture to the saucepan and cook over medium heat, stirring constantly, until it thickens and coats the back of a spoon.
   - Remove from heat and stir in the vanilla extract. Let the custard cool completely.
5. Fill the Profiteroles:
   - Once the profiteroles are cooled, use a sharp knife to cut a small slit in the side of each one.
   - Transfer the cooled custard filling to a piping bag fitted with a small round tip.
   - Pipe the custard into each profiterole until filled.
6. Make the Chocolate Sauce (Optional):
   - In a heatproof bowl set over a pot of simmering water (or in the microwave using short bursts of heat), melt the chopped semisweet chocolate, heavy cream, and butter together, stirring until smooth.
7. Serve:
   - Drizzle the filled profiteroles with the chocolate sauce, if desired.
   - Serve immediately and enjoy!

These custard-filled profiteroles are a delightful dessert, perfect for special occasions or any time you're craving something sweet and indulgent. Enjoy the light, airy pastry filled with creamy custard and decadent chocolate sauce!

Peanut Butter Chocolate Fudge

Ingredients:

- 1 cup creamy peanut butter
- 1 cup semi-sweet chocolate chips
- 1 can (14 ounces) sweetened condensed milk
- 1 teaspoon vanilla extract
- Pinch of salt (optional)

Instructions:

1. Prepare the Pan:
    - Line an 8x8 inch square baking dish with parchment paper, leaving some overhang on the sides for easy removal later.
2. Melt the Peanut Butter and Chocolate:
    - In a medium saucepan over low heat, melt the peanut butter and chocolate chips together, stirring constantly until smooth and well combined.
3. Add Sweetened Condensed Milk:
    - Once the peanut butter and chocolate are melted and smooth, pour in the sweetened condensed milk and stir until fully incorporated.
4. Add Vanilla and Salt:
    - Stir in the vanilla extract and a pinch of salt, if using. The salt enhances the flavors but can be omitted if you prefer.
5. Cook the Fudge Mixture:
    - Continue to cook the mixture over low heat, stirring constantly, for about 3-5 minutes, or until it thickens slightly.
6. Transfer to Pan:
    - Pour the fudge mixture into the prepared baking dish, spreading it out evenly with a spatula.
7. Chill:
    - Place the pan in the refrigerator and chill the fudge for at least 2-3 hours, or until firm and set.
8. Slice and Serve:
    - Once the fudge is completely chilled and set, use the parchment paper overhang to lift it out of the pan.

- Place it on a cutting board and use a sharp knife to cut it into squares or bars.

Enjoy your creamy and decadent peanut butter chocolate fudge! Store any leftovers in an airtight container in the refrigerator for up to a week. It's perfect for sharing with friends and family or for indulging in a sweet treat all to yourself.

Strawberry and Cream Crepes

Ingredients:

For the crepes:

- 1 cup all-purpose flour
- 2 large eggs
- 1 cup milk
- 1/4 cup water
- 2 tablespoons unsalted butter, melted
- 1 tablespoon granulated sugar
- 1 teaspoon vanilla extract
- Pinch of salt

For the filling:

- 1 cup sliced fresh strawberries
- 1 cup whipped cream or whipped topping
- Powdered sugar, for dusting (optional)

Instructions:

1. Prepare the Crepe Batter:
    - In a blender or mixing bowl, combine the flour, eggs, milk, water, melted butter, sugar, vanilla extract, and salt. Blend or whisk until smooth and well combined. Let the batter rest for about 15-30 minutes.
2. Cook the Crepes:
    - Heat a non-stick skillet or crepe pan over medium heat. Lightly grease the pan with butter or cooking spray.
    - Pour about 1/4 cup of the crepe batter into the center of the pan, swirling it around to coat the bottom evenly.
    - Cook the crepe for about 1-2 minutes, or until the edges start to lift and the bottom is lightly golden brown.
    - Flip the crepe using a spatula and cook for an additional 1 minute on the other side. Repeat with the remaining batter, stacking the cooked crepes on a plate as you go.

3. Assemble the Crepes:
    - Lay a crepe flat on a serving plate.
    - Spread a layer of whipped cream evenly over the crepe, leaving a border around the edges.
    - Arrange a layer of sliced strawberries over the whipped cream.
    - Fold the crepe in half, then fold it in half again to form a triangular shape.
    - Repeat with the remaining crepes and filling ingredients.
4. Serve:
    - Dust the filled crepes with powdered sugar, if desired.
    - Serve the strawberry and cream crepes immediately, and enjoy!

These strawberry and cream crepes are delicious served warm or chilled. They're a delightful treat for breakfast, brunch, or dessert, and you can customize them with your favorite fruits and toppings for endless variations.

Honey Joys

Ingredients:

- 4 cups cornflakes
- 90g (3.2 oz) unsalted butter
- 1/3 cup (75g) granulated sugar
- 2 tablespoons honey

Instructions:

1. Preheat Oven and Prepare Muffin Tin:
    - Preheat your oven to 150°C (300°F). Line a 12-cup muffin tin with paper cases.
2. Prepare Cornflakes:
    - Place cornflakes in a large mixing bowl.
3. Melt Butter, Sugar, and Honey:
    - In a saucepan over medium heat, melt the butter, sugar, and honey together, stirring constantly until the sugar is dissolved and the mixture is smooth.
4. Combine Ingredients:
    - Pour the melted butter mixture over the cornflakes. Gently stir until the cornflakes are evenly coated with the mixture.
5. Fill Muffin Cups:
    - Spoon the mixture into the prepared muffin cups, dividing it evenly among them. Press down gently to compact the mixture.
6. Bake:
    - Bake in the preheated oven for 10-12 minutes or until golden brown.
7. Cool and Set:
    - Remove from the oven and let them cool in the tin for a few minutes. Then transfer them to a wire rack to cool completely and set.
8. Serve:
    - Once cooled and set, serve and enjoy these crunchy, sweet Honey Joys!

Honey Joys are perfect for parties, afternoon snacks, or any time you're craving a delicious treat. They're quick to make and always a hit!

www.ingramcontent.com/pod-product-compliance
Lightning Source LLC
LaVergne TN
LVHW081557060526
838201LV00054B/1941